## Praise for The M...

"*The Magic of Connection* offers the reader a wonderful, thorough guide to working with energy. Whether you are seeking practices to support and clear your own energy field, or you need guidance on cutting cords and transmuting energy taken on from others, this book covers it all."
—Alison DeNicola, bestselling author of *Mudras for Awakening the Energy Body*

"In our increasingly fractured world, this modern-day handbook lays out practical tools to freely engage in radical connection with the collective, while healing our own hearts, looking at boundaries in new ways, and by learning to truly transmute the difficult into gold."
—Chris-Anne Donnelly, creator of *The Light Seer's Tarot*, *The Muse Tarot*, and the *Sacred Creators Oracle*

"This book is a nice treatise on the nature of energy and inter-connectedness while also being a how-to manual that guides and informs from the big picture to the granular. Michelle is well-educated in her topic and delivers a fully comprehensive and well-written guide that many will return to over and over again."
—Jenna Matlin, MS, author of *Have Tarot Will Party*

"Michelle Welch offers the steps on how to transform energy to be used by us rather than against us … Stop wasting one of your most precious resources and start building the 'you' you want to be."
—Arwen Lynch, author of *Mapping the Hero's Journey*

"Michelle Welch provides a wealth of information on how to work harmoniously with energy so that we are strengthened and enhanced, rather than diminished and exhausted."
—Ethony Dawn, author of *Your Tarot Court* and headmistress at www.tarotreadersacademy.com

"*The Magic of Connection* walks the reader through simple yet effective steps to regain their own personal power. It is a gem of information that Michelle Welch captures and beautifully shares with the reader."
—Toni Puhle, author of *The Card Geek's Guide to Kipper Cards*

"Michelle Welch invites her readers to look beyond the quick fix, love and light lens and instead intentionally alter our experience with the *Magic of Connection*'s empowering techniques that promote lasting, over temporary, change."
—Carrie Paris, CarrieParis.com

"Michelle Welch's comprehensive and clear explanations and practices provide new insights into how we can protect and strengthen our own energy—something that is so very needed during these difficult times."

—Ruth Ann Amberstone, director of the Tarot School

"*The Magic of Connection* trains empaths to become superheroes. This book is a complete program that takes you from being fearful of your gift to transmuting it into something amazing."

—Jaymi Elford, author of *Tarot Inspired Life* and the *Triple Goddess Tarot*

"We are pretty good at transforming, but Michelle encourages us to reach deeper, toward transmutation. With elegant reasoning, all-too-relatable examples, and achievable exercises, Michelle shows us how to create lasting, healing change."

—Barbara Moore, author of *Modern Guide to Energy Clearing*

"This is a psychic spiritual bootcamp filled with intense training and exercises. Michelle Welch invites you to take a leap of faith and dive into your own waters bringing out all your hidden super-power abilities. She eloquently succeeds in sharing her rich wisdom and teaching the power of transmutation."

—Rana George, author of *The Essential Lenormand* and creator of the *Rana George Lenormand*

"Michelle Welch has tackled a mountain of seemingly difficult information and expressed it in a delightful manner that can be processed and applied for healthy living in a stressful world."

— Susan Lawton, RN, PhD, author of *Living Healthy and Happily Ever After*

"This is an important guidebook for sensitives and empaths (which is all of us, as Michelle points out!) *The Magic of Connection* is chock full of metaphysical wisdom."

—Monte Farber & Amy Zerner, bestselling authors of *The Enchanted Tarot*

"Whether you cast spells, work with the law of attraction, or are simply interested in dealing with those pesky blocks in your life, the principles (and handy tips and tricks) that she reveals in this book will give you the mindset shift you need."

—Madame Pamita, author of *The Book of Candle Magic*

# the MAGIC

## of CONNECTION

## About the Author

Michelle Welch (Dallas, TX) is the owner and operator of the SoulTopia LLC metaphysical stores, where she provides intuitive readings and healing sessions in addition to teaching classes on crystals, tarot, energy work, and intuition. She has also presented at Readers Studio, the Northwest Tarot Symposium, and the International New Age Trade Show. A former lawyer, Michelle is also the host of the *SoulWhat* podcast and the Michelle SoulTopia YouTube channel. Visit her at www.michellewelch.com.

## To Write to the Author

If you wish to contact the author or would like more information about this book, please write to the author in care of Llewellyn Worldwide Ltd. and we will forward your request. Both the author and publisher appreciate hearing from you and learning of your enjoyment of this book and how it has helped you. Llewellyn Worldwide Ltd. cannot guarantee that every letter written to the author can be answered, but all will be forwarded. Please write to:

Michelle Welch
℅ Llewellyn Worldwide
2143 Wooddale Drive
Woodbury, MN 55125-2989
Please enclose a self-addressed stamped envelope for reply,
or $1.00 to cover costs. If outside the U.S.A., enclose
an international postal reply coupon.

Many of Llewellyn's authors have websites with additional
information and resources. For more information,
please visit our website at http://www.llewellyn.com.

Llewellyn Publications
Woodbury, Minnesota

# the MAGIC
## of CONNECTION

Stop Cutting Cords & Learn to
*Transform Negative Energy*
to Live an Empowered Life

# MICHELLE WELCH
## Foreword by Benebell Wen

FIRST EDITION
First Printing, 2021

Cover design by Shira Atakpu
Interior art by Mary Ann Zapalac

Llewellyn Publications is a registered trademark of Llewellyn Worldwide Ltd.

**Library of Congress Cataloging-in-Publication Data**
Names: Welch, K. Michelle, author.
Title: The magic of connection : stop cutting cords & learn to transform
   negative energy to live an empowered life / Michelle Welch.
Description: First edition. | Woodbury, Minnesota : Llewellyn Worldwide,
   Ltd, 2020. | Includes bibliographical references and index. | Summary:
   "For those who already consider themselves to be empaths as well as
   those who want to tap into their empathic side, this book explains how
   to work with the energies that connect all people and, instead of
   cutting energetic cords, teaches readers to transmute challenging
   energies in ways that support their personal spiritual journey. With
   hands-on instructions for using meditations, mantras, crystals, herbs,
   and oils, the book teaches readers how to embrace spiritual connection
   and live a more empowered life. The author includes techniques for
   working with ascended masters, archangels, tarot cards, and more"—
   Provided by publisher.
Identifiers: LCCN 2020041295 (print) | LCCN 2020041296 (ebook) | ISBN
   9780738766706 (paperback) | ISBN 9780738766935 (ebook)
Subjects: LCSH: Magic. | Sensitivity (Personality trait)—Miscellanea. |
   Empathy—Miscellanea. | Extrasensory perception.
Classification: LCC BF1621 .W37 2020  (print) | LCC BF1621 (ebook) | DDC
   133.4/3—dc23
LC record available at https://lccn.loc.gov/2020041295
LC ebook record available at https://lccn.loc.gov/2020041296

Llewellyn Publications
A Division of Llewellyn Worldwide Ltd.
2143 Wooddale Drive
Woodbury, MN 55125-2989
www.llewellyn.com

Printed in the United States of America

## Dedication

To the one bullied for singing sensitive songs
to the one ridiculed for wearing an eye patch
and to the one left out for digging for dinosaurs

# Contents

# Exercises

## Disclaimer

Anyone reading this book or listening to it in any form hereby acknowledges and is tacitly assumed to have read this disclaimer. This publication contains the opinions and ideas of the author. The information provided herein cannot be given to any degree of certainty or guarantee, and you should not rely on it to make any decision that would affect your legal, financial, or medical condition. If any condition, inquiry or situation involves the law, finance, or medicine, then you should seek the advice of a licensed or qualified legal, financial, or medical professional. These methods can only facilitate how you cope spiritually with a given situation. Furthermore, certain jurisdictions require that those in the field of psychic or fortune-telling must state "for entertainment purposes only." To the extent you live in such a jurisdiction, consider yourself on notice thereof. The author and publisher and all of their affiliates specifically disclaim all responsibility for any liability, loss, or risk, personal or otherwise, that is incurred as a consequence, directly or indirectly, of the use and application of any of the contents of this book.

# Foreword

When I was a child, my mother taught me a mantra to Kuan Yin, which she instructed me to repeat while I envisioned golden light spun into a cocoon around me, with enough girth to envelop my auric field. That way, all that passes through and emanates out will transmute to beneficence. Devotional exercises to transmute energy have made all the difference in my life.

In this book, Michelle Welch is going to be teaching you similar, powerful methods of psychic protection. More importantly, *The Magic of Connection* is an invaluable handbook on how to navigate the many energy cords we get hooked by. One of the most important practices for any spiritualist to master is transmutation of social energy, because if you don't change these energies of contact, then the energies will change you, and in discordant situations, change you for the worse.

I'm an occult author, deck creator, tarot reader, astrologer, feng shui consultant and, like Michelle, a lawyer. With the broad spectrum of social interactions I encounter daily, I want to be mindful of my cords of connection. Pernicious ties leave lingering effects that can compound if left unaddressed and, in turn, alter mental and emotional health. That is why a book like *The Magic of Connection* is so important for spiritual hygiene and wellness.

You will often hear modern mystics advise on cord cutting, but as Michelle will tell you, that only works on a temporary basis. Cord cutting is not unlike snipping at the stem of a weed. Those cords will grow back again, spread themselves wider, and more weeds will grow in your garden. You don't actually banish the energy through cord cutting; you've simply compelled it to scatter. That scattering of toxic energy will take root in unexpected places, causing pain in ways that may take you off guard. It's how a scent can trigger troubling past memories and disempower you from being fully present. It's why you lash out at an innocent stranger when three words he speaks remind you of a lover who broke your heart. Those three words had formed cords of connection that you may have thought you cut but had failed to transmute.

Instead, as Michelle phrases it, be the human black tourmaline. The wisest solution may appear counterintuitive at first: absorb all of the energy like black tourmaline. That way you've trapped it in whole. Then visualize white light to transmute that energy, in effect metamorphizing the cord. You're not banishing it; you're fundamentally changing its imprint. Mastery over the techniques you'll learn throughout these chapters will have lasting positive results for your spiritual health. Then, past memories, even when triggered, do not trigger you because you've transmuted them, so their effects are now neutralized.

You are holding in your hands an impressive, judicious text on inner alchemy. Read it through once. Then read it again, many times over to help you better navigate our social world.

Michelle Welch is a friend and fellow attorney. She is the proprietor of SoulTopia, LLC, a metaphysical shop with storefronts in Dallas and Carrollton, Texas. Beyond that, she is a kindred spirit, one of the most compassionate, warm-hearted, and charitable individuals you will encounter. She possesses both an intuitive and sharp empirical understanding of people—their cultures and impulses—which is why she is uniquely positioned to help you maneuver social energy bonds. You will get an expert, balanced, systematic approach to psychic attunements and holistic healing of mind, body, and spirit.

At a Pagan conference one year, two individuals walked into an elevator with me. One remarked delightfully to the other about how so many oblivious and naïve conference attendees were not shielding, and thus their energies were ripe for the taking. They giggled, gleeful and mischievous, at the delicious auric fields for psychic vampires like themselves to feast on. I recount the story because people like that are not unheard of, and you have to be mindful of those who seek to manipulate you, either socially or psychically.

You'll find a chapter in this book on divine guides for transmuting energy. Using similar techniques, in my corner of the elevator that day, I silently evoked a beneficent divinity and asked that she stay close to those two, the self-proclaimed energy vampires I was riding the elevator with, and to be their way-shower, to transmute the energies passing between their cords in ways that will best procreate a greater good. Psychic vampires are who they are and do what they do because of a lack mentality. To transmute their energies, the alchemist must address that lack mentality.

There is no denying the reality that in both the mundane material and psychic realms there will be those who delight in exploiting the vulnerable, so you have to be alert and always one step ahead of others. The way to do that is to be the better alchemist. It isn't enough to simply divert those toxic bearings so they have no impact on you; the empath, the spiritualist, and the kindred spirit are those who will transmute that energy, so it does not cause further decay in our world. That is Michelle Welch's message and the true purpose for your discovery and manifestation of personal power: "We are superheroes with compassion as our capes."

When New Age mystics talk about cords, they're echoing what behavioral psychologists call attachment theory. We form constructive emotional bonds with those who can offer us safety, security, or who, we believe, can help to enhance our wellbeing in some way. Those emotional bonds are essentially positive cords of connection. Thus, one of the first misconceptions that this book dispels is the common notion that cords are negative. They're not. In many instances, our cords are positive.

Attachment theory also explains fear-filled and avoidant bonds caused by insecurity, where life experiences such as abandonment, abuse, or scarcity results in negative attachments. Likewise, negative psychic cords can form from hate, because hate is an emotional bond. But what exactly is hate toward another? When someone expresses hatred of you, they're actually expressing hatred of themselves (and loving what you represent). By realizing that, you can transmute the energy they direct toward you into mercy. Hate is the result of someone seeing you as a threat (which means you're someone so powerful and influential as to pose a threat) or who envies you (which means people see you as blessed and successful). Love and hate are two sides of the same coin. The energy alchemist can flip that coin to land love side facing up.

The psychology of cutting a negative cord tends to result in an unwanted dispersion of that toxic energy elsewhere. It's like cutting an artery. You're rupturing it and discharging that flow of negativity to spray out. Through the inner magic that this book will teach, you will master techniques for siphoning that energy and welcoming it as constructive. For instance, in cords of connection forged by hatred, you will learn how the negativity that someone feels for you is a testament to the power and influence you exude, and of your success. By renaming that energy, you are transmuting hatred into self-love. And when you truly love yourself, all that you send out into the world will be productive and supportive of others.

*The Magic of Connection* comes to us at a time when we as a society are in need of guidance on how to approach the many interpersonal and environmental energies that connect us, but presents these principles in an approach that is wise and compassionate. The most laudable aspect of this book is its steadfast message of kindness toward others, even those who don't behave in ways we understand. When you've let someone else's personality or behavior challenge you, even when you didn't mean for them to have an impact on you, a cord of connection forms. Michelle is the astute and sage teacher who steps forward and shows you how to deal with that cord in a way that restores your wellness and also minimizes harm to the greater collective.

After the unprecedented global COVID-19 pandemic, we've learned just how interconnected all of us are, whether we realize it or not. As powerful as you are in your own personal right, you can just as easily be helpless and vulnerable to the choices other people make, to the energies unknowingly transferred from stranger to stranger. We learned about the profundity of personal responsibility. *The Magic of Connection* enlightens us on the psychic byproducts of interpersonal synergy, both positive and negative.

From Michelle Welch, you will learn how to perceive the network of connections that sustain you and when those cords could potentially be negative, and you will learn many versatile methods for converting negative cords into positive kinetic forces to enrich rather than harm. After all, whether a cord is positive or negative is but a matter of perception. From mantras and meditation work to divine guides, spirit animals, crystals, herbs, incense, and activating the four elements, *The Magic of Connection* is your essential guide to personal—and interpersonal—energy healing.

–BENEBELL WEN
Author of *Holistic Tarot* and *The Tao of Craft: Fu Talismans and Casting Sigils in the Eastern Esoteric Tradition*; creator of the *Spirit Keeper's Tarot*

# Introduction

How often has someone told us *shake it off, get a grip, move on, get over it, let it go, you're too sensitive*, or *toughen up*, only for these platitudes to make us feel worse than we already did? Our friends, family, and society act as if this should be easy—*just let it go for God's sake*. Eventually, the advice may take an even nastier turn. The recommendations are prevalent on social media, where we are encouraged to block, unfriend, and unfollow those we feel have wronged us. Cutting people off on social media is the technological equivalent to cutting cords. Once we follow this advice, we have cut that person out of our life. Or have we? While the painful connection may seem successfully severed for a time, we eventually realize we are still struggling with letting go of these emotions and disconnecting from the perceived negative energy.

For far too long, we have been misled into believing we have to continually safeguard ourselves from all negativity. To protect and deflect, we put up bubbles, boundaries, barriers, and anything else we hope will keep us safe from the evil in the world. These tools, while useful, are defensive measures. If we always play defense, we will never move into the more offensive position of changing the form of the energy, which will fully equip us. It is time we realize that although we may often effectively protect against and deflect energy, eventually, we will absorb it. *The Magic of Connection* helps us learn to mold absorbed energy, thereby transforming any perceived negative energy into a form of energy we can use to live empowered lives.

## What Is This Book About?

*The Magic of Connection* helps us understand we are all energy and, therefore, all connected. As interconnected, empathic beings, we feel into one another and absorb one another's energy. This book introduces many exercises and tools to help us deal with this energy. It includes tools for the beginner that are helpful (even if we never advance beyond that level) to learn the magic we have at our disposal. However, it is essential to know that most tools for protection and deflection only work for a short time, inevitably diminishing in effectiveness and taking us right back to square one. It is an endless cycle of wash, rinse, and repeat. In this book, we will learn we can all become superheroes and transmute energy to help ourselves and others live mighty and dynamic lives on our terms. This book also includes many exercises and tools to advance our transmuting abilities.

Transmuting energy is the magical process of changing the form of energy. It is often referred to as alchemy. While transformation is an integral part of transmutation, the two are different. When we transform energy, the energy remains the same. It merely takes a different form. Transforming is adding dye to water to make it look like wine, while true transmutation is changing water into wine. Transmutation is a complete and total altering of the energy.

The process of alchemy is not foreign to those who practice ceremonial transmutation. However, if disclosed to others, the information is often conveyed in complex and esoteric ways that are often couched in secretiveness and only made available to certain chosen ones. Therefore, transmutation and alchemy have often proven difficult to decipher, hard for many to understand, and often seemingly unattainable.

We are all capable of transmutation, but that does not mean it is easy. *The Magic of Connection* breaks transmutation down into an understandable and relatable process that, with diligence, may be implemented in everyday life. Once we learn to transmute energy we will still utilize protective tools, but ultimately, we will learn to instantaneously transmute energy. The ability to spontaneously transmute energy will help us lose our need to always come from a defensive and even powerless standpoint. Furthermore, we will no longer need to cut cords. We will heal cords through transmutation.

Many of us are familiar with Joseph Campbell's hero's journey introduced in his book *The Hero with a Thousand Faces*. The hero's journey is a metaphor for the journey of transformation all heroes go through. There are three primary levels of the journey. In this book, we will follow the Superhero's Journey through the three levels empaths traverse. For our purposes, these levels will include: Unequipped Empath, Empath in Training, and Equipped Empath. As we progress, we learn to put away our emotional shields and put on our energetic capes. These levels will help us understand how to proceed from absorbing energy to ultimately transmuting energy.

## Who Am I to Question Cord Cutting?

Over years of practicing law and serving as an energy worker, healer, medical intuitive, and psychic medium, plus owning two metaphysical stores, one thing is overwhelmingly apparent to me. Many people, including myself, are often desperate to move on from relationships or situations they deem negative. I have observed countless cases of clients with different circumstances, yet the same underlying issue. They remain stuck in a perpetual cycle of trying to avoid any energy that causes them pain. For a time, tools such as bubbles of protection, mirrors, and even walls seem effective, but over time the effectiveness wanes. Ultimately, the clients come to me at their wits' end. They have tried everything to escape the opposition. Eventually, many attempt a process called cord cutting.

Cord cutting is a process that encourages severing cords—energy ties between people, places, things, or situations—through visualization or other types of energy work. An energy healer often facilitates the cord cutting. The idea is to help people let go when they are having trouble doing so. In theory, once the cord is cut, they should have no attachment to the energy. However, I notice from courtroom proceedings to energy healings this process never works because cords always reattach. For years this has caused me to question the whole process. I also recount all the occasions when I suggested different tools to help someone let go of the things and people that hurt them.

The most frequently suggested tool is perhaps a black tourmaline. Black tourmaline is a type of crystal known to absorb, deflect, and transmute negative energy. After recommending this to countless clients, one day it hit me like the rock that it is (pun intended): if a black tourmaline can do these things, why can't we? We have all absorbed energy, deflected energy, and protected against energy. Why can't we transmute energy? I have written this book to challenge all of us to finally step into our roles as superheroes of transmutation of energy.

## Who Will Benefit from This Book?

Everyone can benefit from this book. In fact, this book is needed now more than ever. In this hurting world, it is time for us to realize our ability to sense our oneness with others and, therefore, our ability to feel others' energy so that we may begin our Superhero's Journey. Many of us do not want to heed our call to adventure. Often, we will sense energy that does not feel in alignment with ours. In other words, it may feel negative or unwanted. There are varying degrees to which we feel this energy. Some of us feel and take on other energy as if it were directly our own. "Other energy" encompasses all energy, both living and nonliving. For the purposes of this book, those of us who take on other energy as if it were our own will be referred to as traditional empaths. Others may seem oblivious to the energy. Many believe that those who are not aware of the energy they are feeling are not empaths. However, even though some may not recognize that they feel others' energy, they feel it and absorb it, which makes them, by definition, an empath. We all just experience energy differently.

Those of us who have been labeled as traditional empaths—whether by a psychologist or an online blog quiz—are those who are often aware that we feel energy more consistently and acutely than others. The majority of us possess few skills regarding how to deal with our sensitivities to other energies because we have received little to no training. While we are facing our call to adventure on our Superhero's Journey, we need tools to help us protect against energies that may harm us.

While this book may address those who identify more profoundly as empaths, it is beneficial for everyone, whether they relate as a traditional empath or not. It is crucial in this complex world that we all begin to realize how to deal with our empathic natures. Even if it is difficult to see it in yourself, it is probably easy to recognize it in someone else. We may have children, friends, or clients we work with that can benefit from the concepts introduced in this book.

*The Magic of Connection* will guide us through each phase of learning to transmute energy. The end goal is to transmute energy in the moment. However, getting to that point does not usually happen overnight. This book includes step-by-step exercises and tools to help us understand how we process energy. These exercises are helpful for everyone, from young children to mature adults. The more we use the activities and tools, the more we will find we can manage and transform energy, thereby empowering our lives. When we realize empaths are superheroes, we will shake off the conditioned belief that we are too sensitive to handle other energy. We will change the form of how we experience our energy and how we transform other energy. As superheroes, we also have at least one sidekick and many different mentors and teachers to help us along our Superhero's Journey. *The Magic of Connection* helps us every step of the way from our call to adventure to our complete transformation, without the need to cut cords, but instead heal the energy of us all.

## What Topics Will Be Covered in This Book?

To better understand how to deal with energy more effectively in our lives, we must first understand energy and how we are all connected to that energy. To help, we will walk through fundamental principles known as the laws of the universe. Once we understand how energy works, we need to understand how we each deal with that energy.

We will also dive into how we are all empaths in one way or another. We will begin our Superhero's Journey to learn to tap into our gifts for the greater good. Many forms of protection from unwanted energy are covered, because most of us have not fully learned to transmute energy. We will also meet sidekicks and tools along our Superhero's Journey to assist us, such as crystals, affirmations, spirit guides, animal guides, herbs, candles, and tarot. When purchasing any of these tools, asking where the items are sourced is always a good idea to ensure that they are ethically and legally obtained. Through exercises in each chapter, these sidekicks and tools will help us develop our transmuting abilities so that we do not need to cut cords. Then we can put on our superhero capes and take the final and most important leap in our journey. We will transmute energy.

## How Should This Book Be Used?

In order for us to fully grasp and properly execute the totality of the concepts conveyed in *The Magic of Connection*, it is best utilized by reading and practicing the exercises that are included in each chapter. Even if we are an advanced energy worker or alchemist, we can benefit from performing all of the exercises. Doing so provides us a fresh look at our energy and how we connect with others. The exercises throughout the book build on one another and may seem similar. This similarity helps us enter a meditative state more quickly as we advance through the book. We can approach these exercises in any manner that feels right to us, including rewording them to fit our belief systems when necessary.

Journaling is also recommended. This is one of the best ways to become aware of our own energy. Once we know what energy belongs to us, we can more easily distinguish it from someone else's energy. Journaling helps us recognize our growth on our Superhero's Journey. Our journal may also serve as a map to help guide us when we face similar issues in the future. Writing need not intimidate us. Even jotting down a few thoughts or ideas can benefit us along our path.

Because many concepts are covered in *The Magic of Connection,* it is broken into two easily digestible parts: The Superhero's Call to Adventure and The Superhero's Tools and Sidekicks. Part One: The Superhero's Call to Adventure, helps us understand who we really are, how we are all connected, why this oneness changes our views on cords, and what we can do to step into a new way of thinking and living even while still employing tools we may have used in the past. Part Two: The Superhero's Tools and Sidekicks, introduces us to affirmations, mantras and meditations, spirit guides, animal guides, crystals, herbs, incense, essential oils, candles, spells, and tarot sidekicks to help us as we grow from absorbing and deflecting energy into realizing and practicing transmutation of energy. Each chapter contains exercises to help us on our journey to becoming the masters and magicians of energy. This book helps us transform our lives and thereby the lives of everyone through the process of transmutation. This process will be thoroughly explained to us each step of the way. We are challenged to step into our call to adventure, stop limiting ourselves, and enjoy our journey into *The Magic of Connection*.

# Part One

# The Superhero's Call to Adventure

*"When you follow your bliss, and by bliss I mean the deep sense of being in it, and doing what the push is out of your own existence—it may not be fun, but it's your bliss and there's bliss behind pain too."* — Joseph Campbell[1]

1.  Joseph Campbell. *The Hero's Journey: The World of Joseph Campbell: Joseph Campbell on His Life and Work* (United Kingdom: HarperSanFrancisco, 1991), 214.

*Chapter One*

# The Big Dysfunctional Collective

*Everything Is Energy,*
*and Everything Is Connected*

G rowing up, I would often go waterskiing. The lake I skied on was so smooth it looked like glass. I remember I could skip a rock on the lake, and it would cause ripples on the water as far as I could see. Eventually, the ripples would hit something and bounce back toward me. The more important things that would create ripples were other boats. The boat wakes were large ripples extending out from the motion of the boat in the water. The boat wakes could knock a skier down. However, a more advanced skier would take advantage of the wakes and learn to jump them. But whether the cause was a little rock or a large boat, there would always be a ripple effect. Anything that occurred in the lake affected everything else in the lake and beyond on some level. In the same way, everything we think and do exponentially affects the world, universe, and beyond.

In this increasingly complex and divisive society, it is more important than ever to understand our potential to affect others and to understand the ripple effect our words and actions have on everyone and everything. Most of us have heard of this ripple effect, but how often have we really stopped to think about the power of an emotional ripple effect? I think of the times I was made fun of as the skinny, ugly girl in physical education class. The emotional ripple effect often was not one of kindness. The more girls that heard the derision, the more the insults came from other sources. When it rained, we would be left mostly unattended in the gymnasium. About ten girls would gather around me on the bleachers and their taunting knew no bounds. *You are ugly and too skinny, but maybe someday you will be pretty because your mother is pretty*. If I dared try to say anything to defend myself, I would simply be told *you are too sensitive*. This ripple effect carried over to the school bus where I now know I was the victim of verbal, emotional, and sexual abuse. Yet for some reason, in the midst of my pain, I was always kind to others who I felt were hurting more. I was kind to those sitting alone or to those who were mentally or physically challenged. Then, of course, I was ridiculed for that as well. I was *too sensitive*. I would catch myself even having pity for the people who made fun of me because I knew something had to be horribly sad in their lives to act in such a way. At times, I still struggle with the words that I have now learned to say in response to those who do not understand us sensitives, but I hope we all know them by the end of this book. The words are: *Thank You! No, not for bullying me—but thank you for calling me sensitive because I am changing the world. Thank you, and would you like to join me?*

Today, people seem to think that it is acceptable to advocate hatred. There is a lot of talk of lines in the sand and cutting people off if they do not believe the way we believe. I hear less and less talk of healing, forgiveness, and most importantly, oneness. In times like these, we desperately need to understand our potential to transmute energy to change the world. We are about to embark upon a Superhero's Journey, which consists of three levels. For our purposes, these levels will include Unequipped Empath, Empath in Training, and Equipped Empath. These levels will help us understand how to proceed from absorbing energy to ultimately transmuting energy.

However, before we can understand how to step into our transmutation superpowers, it is imperative to understand our importance and interconnectedness to one another. When the internet first came about, everyone was confident it would bring the world together. We would no longer feel isolated or alone. We would all be connected by the World Wide Web. However, over time, we began to notice a shift. It seemed people, including younger generations, were isolating behind their computer or technology screens. The need for face-to-face interaction was speculated to be in danger of becoming obsolete. Everything could take place from behind a screen with no real interaction with humans. However, when faced with a need for social distancing, the world found out just how much we needed human contact. We realized how connected we really were and how much we craved the socialization of the connection. The time of necessary social distancing became an unprecedented study in not only connecting with other energy from a distance but also how we, as humans, crave the personal interaction and energy between humans. After years and years of evolution, our instinct tells us we are safer around other humans. Whether it be a hundred thousand years ago around a campfire or today around the dinner table, we need one another. We are not separate; we are connected and were designed to function as such.

To understand who we are, how we interact with others, and how we are all connected, we first must comprehend a few underlying principles. We may have heard many spiritual catchphrases along our soul's journey, such as *we are all one; as above, so below;* or *you create your reality.* Many times, we find ourselves accepting these oft-repeated phrases, perhaps without really understanding their meanings. To fully understand ourselves and our connection with others, it is essential to have not only some awareness but also a basic grasp of these words and phrases.

Let us consider some of these concepts. For those of you that find these concepts elementary, simply read them to see if you gain a new perspective. For the rest of us, let's try to break them down. Within the laws of the universe, we find areas where science and spirituality often overlap. There are specific laws of the universe and scientific laws that affect us at all times, whether or not we realize it. If we step back and look at our lives, we begin to see how these apply. If we work within these laws instead of fighting against them, we will find ourselves riding the waves of life instead of crashing into them. For ease of understanding, here is a list of some of the laws of the universe and other scientific principles that we will address. While we will not get bogged down in these principles, we need to become aware of them.

1. Everything is energy

2. Law of Conservation of Energy

3. The Collective

4. Law of Divine Oneness

5. Law of Vibration

6. Law of Correspondence

7. Law of Attraction

8. Law of Inspired Action

9. Law of Perpetual Transmutation of Energy

10. Law of Cause and Effect

11. Law of Compensation

12. Law of Relativity

13. Law of Polarity

14. Law of Rhythm

15. Entanglement Theory

Let's start with who and what we are: everything is energy. Understanding this concept will ultimately help us overcome our illusion of separateness and help us begin to understand our connectivity. We have probably all heard this at some point. But what does this short, matter-of-fact statement mean, and why does it matter? This proclamation, although seemingly simple, is actually quite complex. In fact, Einstein was asked what he wanted to know most about physics. He replied, "I would just like to know what an electron is."[2] So, of course, the simple phrase everything is energy is more complicated than it seems. Einstein, speaking about the relationship between matter and energy, said, "It follow[s] from the special theory of relativity that mass and energy are both but different manifestations of the same thing—

2.   Cate, Montana, *The E-Word: Ego, Enlightenment & Other Essentials* (New York: Atria/Enliven Books, 2017), 111; Milo Wolff and Geoff Haselhurst, "Light and the Electron—Einstein's Last Question," (presentation at Beyond Einstein, Stanford University, May 2004), https://www-conf.slac.stanford.edu/einstein/talks/wolff.pdf.

a somewhat unfamiliar conception for the average mind."[3] Simply put, since everything in the universe has mass, everything, therefore, is energy.

Now that we understand that everything is energy, we can begin to look at some fundamental laws, principles, and theories of the universe. Not only is everything energy, but the Law of Conservation of Energy also states that energy never goes away; it just changes form. This law is important and central to transmutation. There is a set amount of energy, and it never goes away. It merely changes form. The Law of Divine Oneness states that we are all connected in The Collective. When we think of ourselves as part of one body, we begin to treat everyone and everything differently and, hopefully, with more understanding. Everything in The Collective is always moving and has its own energy frequency, as set forth in the Law of Vibration.

The Law of Vibration states that everything is in a continual state of movement or vibration. The speed of the vibrations makes things appear to be liquid, solid, or gas. Words, like everything else in the universe, have vibrations. It is important to remember that everything vibrates at different frequencies or rates of vibration. Because the frequencies are different, we notice discrepancies in other forms of energy, including other people. These vibrations may feel low or they may feel high. A lower vibration is denser and feels more substantial. A higher vibration is more etheric and feels lighter. At some point, we begin to label vibrations as low energy or high energy. These frequencies are much like radio channels. Some music will vibe with us, while other music will not. We can change the radio channel to select the frequency we enjoy or is in alignment with how we feel and what we believe. However, it is essential to know that while we may change the radio channel, every sound in the universe is still heard and felt on some level.

The Law of Correspondence is most often known by the phrases *as within, so without* or *as above, so below*. It means that our outer world is an expression of our inner world. Meaning that as we think we will be, but more importantly, as we communicate or correspond with ourselves, we will be. This law is fundamental because it requires us to take responsibility for our

---

3.  "Einstein Explains the Equivalence of Energy and Matter," The Center for History of Physics, transcribed from *Atomic Physics*, J. Arthur Rank Organization, 1948, https://history.aip.org/history/exhibits/einstein/voice1.htm.

energy and life. The Law of Correspondence requires us to mind our own energy.

The Law of Attraction teaches us that like attracts like regarding energy frequencies, but it is also important to know there is a Law of Inspired Action, which means we enthusiastically seek that which awakens or stirs something within us. The word action is contained within the word attraction. We can attempt to manifest something such as the ideal job, but we must put some effort behind it instead of just sitting on our couch and waiting for things to happen. The Law of Perpetual Transmutation of Energy states that everything is always changing even though we might not always be able to see it. Therefore, not only does energy never go away according to the Law of Conservation of Energy, but it also changes form. It is encouraging and helpful to realize we can change the form of energy, which is the ultimate step called transmutation. Transmutation is the magic we fall short of achieving but will learn in this book. The Law of Perpetual Transmutation of Energy provides us with our superhero's mantra: we are transmuters of energy.

The Law of Cause and Effect simply states that all actions have a corresponding reaction. According to the Law of Compensation, what we radiate will return to us in unexpected ways. This seems a lot like the Law of Attraction, but while it sometimes may relate to money, it is usually more about feelings, thoughts, and ideas. Do you feel resented? Chances are, you are resentful toward someone else. Do you feel appreciated? Chances are, you are showing appreciation to others.

The Law of Relativity emphasizes that there is no distinction without comparison. We may think we are treated unjustly until we see and acknowledge the plight of a truly disenfranchised fellow human. Everything can be looked at from multiple perspectives. This law is particularly relevant to why we transmute rather than cut cords. Who are we to stand in judgment of someone else's energy? Instead, when we transmute, we are lifting the vibration for The Collective.

The Law of Polarity reminds us that everything has two opposing forces, or a flipside. If we have never experienced any sadness at losing a friend, for example, we may not fully appreciate what it means to have a friend. The Universal Law of Polarity reminds us that if there is positive energy, there is negative energy. If there is light, there is darkness. If there is happiness, there is sadness. All of these states of being, or energy, really come down to how we label them. They are opposite ends of the same spectrum. Yet, again, it is one spectrum. It is one energy. One person may label something positive, and another person will label the same thing negative, as we learned from the Law of Relativity. Much of what we feel comes from how we label energy. How we label the energy often comes from our experiential filters. We hear time and time again to be mindful of our thoughts and words because we will manifest that reality. Those thoughts and words are energy, and all energy is in a constant state of vibration.

The Law of Perpetual Motion, also known as the Law of Rhythm, is that all things come in successive phases like seasons, nothing is static. This is the great pendulum of life, or, the idea that we are moving forward or moving backward. There is no standing still. When we begin to gain mastery over our energies, we will realize that there will always be ebbs and flows in life.

Although we are all one, as in all one collective, does this mean we are all one big happy family? No, it does not. Well, why not? We know, from the Law of Vibration, that energy vibrates at different frequencies. We also know, from the Law of Relativity, that this energy may feel different to those experiencing it. This experiential difference in sensing energy will vary from one person to another. This ultimately leads to labeling the energy as positive or negative and everything in between. Although the labeling of energy does serve some purposes, such as helping determine social mores and laws of society, the judgments that come with the experiential labeling of energy are where we often find ourselves in the throes of disagreement. How to deal with this dilemma rears its head time and time again throughout *The Magic of Connection*. As we ascertain what energy we want to transmute, a certain amount of labeling and judgment will undoubtedly take place.

As we begin to understand the Law of Correspondence, we may realize that some of the energy directed at us from the outside that we perceive as negativity is actually mirroring. It is mirroring back to us what we need to change in ourselves. When we meet other people, we can think of them as a mirror of ourselves. If we smile at others, they typically smile back at us. However, if we are rude, the other person might reciprocate with aloofness. Remember, we are all connected, and we serve as mirrors to one another. Let us consider disagreements as another example. Keep in mind, the next time we get in an argument, we are, at least in part, arguing with ourselves. Perhaps not literally but in theory with another aspect of ourselves. Next, we move into the areas that the scientists and physicists don't even fully understand.

Quantum theory may not sound complicated to everyone, but it does to most of us. Even so, we need to at least scratch the surface of quantum physics to understand our connectivity further. The idea of a life force flowing through everything is not new. But perhaps the most important theory to understand is that of entanglement. Entanglement is the theory that everything is intertwined. It makes no difference how far apart particles are in space or in time; they are connected. From atoms to people, everything responds and communicates with one another.

To begin to put the pieces of our human puzzle together, we must first understand why this is so important in our day-to-day lives. The simple answer is because we are social creatures. We crave connection; isolation is not in our wiring. Unfortunately, it has become increasingly common for many in spiritual practices to encourage cutting us off from anything that causes pain, discomfort, or even irritation. The battle cries fill our minds: *Cut off that which does not serve you! Be your authentic self and remove those who don't agree! Sever ties and cut cords with the assholes in our lives!* We could go on and on. We have all heard these statements, and many of us pick up the battle cries. We have bought into the lie that we should always run from perceived negativity. Let's consider this thought concept. Many believe we have come to this beautiful planet, Mother Earth, to grow and learn. Why then, do we feel the need to protect and cut ourselves off from many of the things and people that enter our lives for such lessons? Spiritual awakening is not all rainbows and unicorns. Perhaps the thought of learning or growing is not always fun; however, it is the reason we often espouse for coming to the earth.

We all have energetic cords connecting us to everything and everyone. All of these cords ultimately connect to Source, or what some may refer to as God, Universe, or Divine. Hopefully, grasping this interconnectedness will lead us to understand our oneness and the misguidance of a concept known as cutting cords. As we recognize our connection to everything and everyone, many of us may dig our heels in and think of reasons why this connection does not apply in every case. In our haste to support our need to protect and cut ourselves away from those with whom we are unhappy, we immediately, and understandably, rush to the worst possible scenarios. We ask, what about the narcissist, abuser, pedophile, or murderer? Do we have to remain entangled with them? After all, we are perfect, and we can assign a scale as to when we do not need someone else in our lives. Right? Well, not really. Because of our recognition of energy and entanglement, we have no choice but to acknowledge our interconnectivity. Yes, the complaints are getting louder now. We can choose to cut ourselves off from whomever we want! Once again, no. We really cannot. We may convince our conscious mind on some level that we have achieved a disconnect, but our subconscious knows. We always know, on some deep level, of our connectedness to everyone and everything. The painful concept of our connectedness to people whose behavior horrifies us will be discussed further in chapter 8.

We have already established that everything in this energy field is vibrating and connected. Of course, knowing that we are all one does not imply we are entirely the same, but instead implies a connection between parts that are not altogether different. We can maintain our autonomy while we are concurrently part of the whole, known as The Collective. All of the unconscious, subconscious, conscious, and superconscious parts of every particle of energy combine to comprise The Collective. It is a living, energetic being composed of All That Is. It is directly connected to Source and includes Source. Just like the ripple effect on the lake, this means that every single thing we think or do affects the whole because we are all one.

## *Exercise*
### Energy Sensing

In order to learn how to transform negative energy to live an empowered life, you must first understand and be able to identify your own energy. The following exercise will help you do just that. Over time, you will progress to sensing other forms of energy besides your own. The more consistently you practice the exercise, the more you will advance. Eventually, you will begin to realize when you are feeling into other forms of energy. You will sense not only the energy of the other forms, but you will sense your oneness with them.

In a quiet and safe space, close your eyes and become still in your body. Begin to become aware of your left hand. It is as if your entire being is now associated with your left hand. Your left hand is your entire being. Notice any sensations you feel in your hand. Breathe and simply notice the sensations. Does your left hand feel warm or cold? Is it heavy or light? Is it tingly or numb? Continue to sense the essence of your left hand for just a moment longer. Now make a fist with your right hand and rub it into the palm of your left hand. You are waking up the mini chakras in your hands called nadis. Nadis connect directly to your heart chakra. These chakras are energy centers. Begin to gently rub or even tap on your left palm with your right fist. Feel the tingling in your left hand. It may begin to grow warmer. When you are ready, place your hands gently in your lap.

Now become aware of your right hand. It is as if your entire being is now associated with your right hand. Your right hand is your entire being. Notice any sensations you feel in your hand. Breathe and simply notice the sensations. Does your right hand feel warm or cold? Is it heavy or light? Is it tingly or numb? Continue to sense the essence of your right hand for just a moment longer. Now make a fist with your left hand and rub it into the palm of your right hand. Once again, you are waking up the mini chakras or energy centers in your hands called nadis. Begin to gently rub or even tap on your right palm with your left fist. Feel the tingling in your hand. It may begin to grow warmer.

Now bring your hands together about two inches apart from one another. Begin to feel the energy flowing from one hand to the other. It may feel like zaps of electricity. It may feel tingly. You may just sense pressure or tension between your two hands. It may feel like a magnet either attracting or repelling your hands. Once you sense the energy, pull your hands just a little farther apart from one another. If at any time you stop feeling the energy, bring your hands closer together. Continue working with the energy between your hands. You can mold the energy into a sphere shape by cupping your hands toward one another. You have created a chi ball holding life force between your hands. The key is to maintain the energetic connection so that you sense and feel it. Explore this energy for a while longer.

Once completed, bring your hands together in front of your heart in a prayerlike position. Give gratitude for any energy you were able to sense.

Ground yourself by feeling the connection from your feet to Mother Earth. You are one with her. Feel energetic roots extending from the bottoms of your feet down into the core of Mother Earth. Wrap the roots around her core and pull some energy back up through your feet and into the rest of your body. Always remember to send some of your gratitude and loving energy through your feet to Mother Earth. Now imagine a place in the cosmos such as a star or a planet. Your higher or soul self may originate from here. Visualize lassoing some of your energy around that star or planet. Give it a little tug. Now you are equally grounded between heaven and earth. When you are ready, bring your attention back into the room and your body. Wiggle your fingers and your toes. When you are ready, slowly and gently open your eyes.

Various techniques to add as you advance:

- When you are ready, and if the energy feels inviting to you, place both of your palms flat on your heart chakra at the center of your chest. The nadis in your hands are connected to your heart chakra. Using the electricity you formed is a beautiful way to calm any anxiety you may feel.
- Try sensing the energy of your feet. The nadis in your feet are attached to your root chakra, located where you sit.
- Try sensing the energy of other living things such as an animal or a plant.
- Try sensing the energy of a crystal.
- Try sensing the energy of an article of clothing.
- Try sensing the energy of furniture.

As you advance in this exercise, you may begin to notice other sensory messages. These sensory messages may include images, feelings, sounds, smells, or tastes coming into your awareness. You are connected to all energy. Expect to feel into the energy to which you are one.

Knowing that we are all one, and more importantly really believing it, will begin to change the way we think and speak not only to ourselves but to others. Realizing we are all one will also change how we treat Mother Earth.

*Exercise*
## Group Oneness

This exercise will help you begin to feel and realize our connectedness to one another and to All That Is. This exercise will require a minimum of two people or up to as many people as you desire. For the sake of organization, you should designate a facilitator before you begin the exercise.

Sit in a circle. Close your eyes and draw your attention to your breath. Begin to slow down your breathing. Open your eyes and turn to the person next to you. Each of you hold up your palms vertically and keep them about two inches away from your partner. Begin to feel the energy between you and your partner's hands. You may feel tingling in your hands or pressure like a magnet. Note what you are feeling. If you are both sensing energy, pull your hands even farther apart as long as you maintain the connection. Begin to form a chi or life force ball with your hands. As long as you hold the connection, you can even toss the energy back and forth. When everyone in the circle is ready, turn back toward the circle.

Close your eyes again and draw your attention to your breath. Once again, begin to slow down your breathing. Hold one palm facing up at your side and the other palm facing down at your other side. The person on each side of you in the circle will do the same. Keep your palms about three inches away from the person on either side. The leader of the group can then announce they are sending energy around the circle clockwise. The energy goes from one person to the next until it has gone around the room. The group can send energy around as many times as they desire.

Once completed, bring your hands together in front of your heart in a prayerlike position. Give gratitude for your connection to the circle. Ground yourself by feeling the connection from your feet to Mother Earth. You are one with her. Feel energetic roots extending from the bottoms of your feet down into the core of Mother Earth. Wrap the roots around her core and pull some energy back up through your feet and into the rest of your body. Always remember to send some of your gratitude and loving energy through your feet to Mother Earth. Now imagine a place in the cosmos such as a star or a planet. Your higher or soul self may originate from here. Visualize lassoing some of your energy around that star or planet. Give it a little tug. Now you are equally grounded between heaven and earth. When you are ready, bring your attention back into the room and your body. Wiggle your fingers and your toes. When you are ready, slowly and gently open your eyes.

## *Exercise*
## Spiderweb Oneness

This exercise will help you begin to feel and realize your connectedness to All That Is.

Close your eyes and draw your attention to your breath. Begin to slow down your breathing. In your mind's eye, take yourself to a safe space. The safe space may be an actual physical place or a place you go in your meditations. You may be on a beach, on a mountaintop, in a field, or in the heavens. Go to a place you find comforting. You find yourself lying on your back. You begin looking up at the sky. The sky is incredibly bright, and it starts as daylight. The sun does not bother your eyes. You feel a cool breeze on your face and know you are safe. As you look at the sky, you begin to see beautiful strands or cords start to appear. They are bright and comfortable to view. The cords start to connect across the sky. They go as far as you can see. You continue to watch everything join, and all of a sudden, you realize the air is a night sky filled with stars. The cords keep connecting like an intricate spiderweb. You feel the oneness of all. The cords are beautiful. They look and feel as if they are perfectly united. You realize that everyone came from stardust. There is no division. You know that you are one with All That Is. Everyone and everything connect to you. You feel whole.

Once completed, bring your hands together in the middle of your chest in a prayerlike position. Give gratitude for your connection to everything and everyone. Ground yourself by feeling the connection from your feet to Mother Earth. You are one with her. Feel energetic roots extending from the bottoms of your feet down into the core of Mother Earth. Wrap the roots around her core and pull some energy back up through your feet and into the rest of your body. Always remember to send some of your gratitude and loving energy through your feet to Mother Earth. Now imagine a place in the cosmos such as a star or a planet. Your higher or soul self may originate from here. Visualize lassoing some of your energy around that star or planet.

Give it a little tug. Now you are equally grounded between heaven and earth. When you are ready, bring your attention back into the room and your body. Wiggle your fingers and your toes. When you are ready, slowly and gently open your eyes.

*Chapter Two*

# Squeezing Out the Sponge
## *Embracing Empathy*

As the owner of two metaphysical stores, I am in a unique position to hear what customers are going through in their lives. Quite possibly, the most common statement I hear in my stores is, *I'm an empath*. Often following this proclamation is a list of things the customer feels they cannot do because they believe everything affects their energy and prevents them from doing those things. This includes giving or receiving hugs, going to large events, being around too many people, or watching the news. Some are even so sensitive to the environment around them that they find it difficult to leave their house at all. The frequency with which I hear these statements, and more, has set me on a quest for answers.

Several issues concern me regarding *empath* as a trending buzzword and the available resources around the topic of empaths. The issues all come down to the fact that most resources fall short of fully equipping empaths. In fact, many are ultimately disempowering. My quest for answers surrounding this topic grows stronger every time I hear someone say they are an empath, and I hear it multiple times a day.

As I stated in the introduction, it is important to remember that everyone *feels into* other energy, which is a combination of feeling and absorbing energy. This feeling into others' energy makes everyone, by definition, an empath. Yes, even those sociopaths who feed on the fear of others absorb and sense energy. Further, although many empaths are compassionate, this trait is not inherent in the truest definition of an empath or even empathy for that matter. The difference is the extent to which we absorb this energy. The difference is also that those of us who identify as empaths already understand, on some level, that we absorb this energy, that we feel and can feel into others. We are traditional empaths.

At this juncture, I wish to emphasize we are all empaths. What varies is (1) the awareness each of us has of the fact that we are absorbing other energies and that we are indeed human sponges—a concept we further explore later in this chapter and (2) the degree of sensitivity with which we react to this energy. Think of the degrees of sensitivity as a continuum, with one end being extremely sensitive and aware of the energy in a situation while the other end might be labeled completely unaware. We all need to understand energy and how to work with it. That is part of this book's purpose: to help us all be able to manage energy at high, empowering levels.

Perhaps the attention drawn to the reality of traditional empaths is necessary. Indeed, I understand many of the feelings of those with empathy pains. In fact, not only do I understand them, I *feel* them because I am a card-carrying traditional empath. However, I must admit, the publicity the subject of empaths receives, and the resulting exploitation, is disconcerting. After all, some empaths are aware from an early age that they are sensitive to energy and learn strategies for dealing with the impact this energy has on us. However, this is not frequently the case. For many traditional empaths, life is a confusing journey until we come across the label of *empath*. This label starts off as an extremely freeing word to us sensitives. We finally have an explanation for why situations and people affect us so deeply. We finally feel understood. We are empaths! We begin to understand that we take on the energy of others. We read books and take quizzes that validate how we feel. We are empaths! Finally, with a label and definition, a wave of information becomes available. But the disturbing trend is that many of us, usually unknowingly, begin to hide behind the label that we are empaths as an excuse for all the reasons we *can't* in the world.

For those of us who identify at the extremely sensitive end of the spectrum, those traditionally labeled as empaths, we should be aware that we have some special challenges on our Superhero's Journey. As superheroes responding to our call to adventure, it is helpful to understand some of the traps along our path so that we can successfully navigate them. Let's examine a few of them.

**Trap 1:** Avoid the emotions of others. Although there is a plethora of materials written for us empaths, most of the blogs, articles, books, and media have fallen short. Why? Because they fail to truly empower and equip us. Instead of helping us realize we are the superheroes needed for a world in pain, this advice—numb yourself to the energy of others, protect yourself, hide, cut yourself off—may actually put us in a perpetual defensive mode. Ultimately, we are disempowered. We try to block out any energy we feel hurts us. In the extreme, a lack of training may lead us to become reclusive, and at its worst, we actually may become suicidal. More defensive measures are certainly helpful on our Superhero's Journey, but eventually a superhero must learn offensive measures. Let us begin to see every empath with superhero capes standing in the power of what we can do instead of what we can't do.

**Trap 2:** Numb our feelings. This is closely related to trap one. There is a tendency for some empaths to mask or numb the pain we pick up from others. The desire to avoid distressing energy is why many traditional empaths struggle with various forms of self-sabotaging habits or addictions. We continue to run from or dull our perceptions, but it does not work. Ultimately, we cannot escape the reality in which we live.

**Trap 3:** Believe the labels. We may have parents, teachers, and even counselors tell us that we need to toughen up. We are often told to *let things go* or to *get over it*. Others mistakenly presume our compassion and caring to be weaknesses. They label us as *too sensitive* or say we care too much. The truth is, many empaths may grow into adulthood never fully understanding why we have this incredible ability to feel into others. Our lack of confidence and our belief in these labels has led some to mistakenly call us *immature empaths*. Rather than being immature, which carries a negative connotation, we empaths are quite mature in our ability. What we are often lacking is proper training in our gift. Believing the labels leads us to not lean into our superpowers. We remain unempowered and hurting.

**Trap 4:** Energy is negative. Almost every writer on the subject of empaths focuses solely on the fact that empaths soak up negative energy. This misplaced focus is illogical because empaths are sensitive to all energies; therefore, they are also aware of the so-called positive energies. This positive energy still needs differentiating, but it does not necessarily need transmuting. Why is the emphasis almost always on the negative? Perhaps it is because when we take on positive energy, we fail to acknowledge it. However, when we take on negative energy, we may feel chronic fatigue, irritableness, anxiety, and more. Therefore, it is just as important to teach an empath to expect positivity as well as negativity. Let us look forward to hearing other empaths speak about the positive energy they sense in a room or a person instead of the tendency to always focus on negative energy.

**Trap 5:** Cut the cord. It is understandable why many traditional empaths are wary of negativity. Many of us have walked on eggshells as long as we can remember. Whether trepidation was due to a critical mother, an alcoholic father, or an abusive teacher, we were on high alert to other energy at a young age. We learned to tiptoe around situations that we innately knew were harmful to us. Many of us have memories of events where something left us feeling as if we would never recover. Those memories might still feel like a punch in the gut every time we think of the situation, especially if we haven't fully processed that energy. This overwhelming feeling is because we are extremely sensitive to energy. Our cording to the situation, person, and memory makes it ludicrous for anyone to attempt to teach an empath to toughen up. It is equally ridiculous to suggest cutting cords with those that hurt us. Why? Because empaths are meant to *feel*. We are intended to *absorb*. However, we are also born to *transmute*. The adage "give it time" begins to grow old. We try, but still, we hold on to the energy. Ultimately, the suggestion comes to cut cords or cut that person or feeling out of our life. But all too often, although we may feel better for a short time, the hurt, anger, and resentment return. Inevitably, we feel as though we are the weak ones. We are not confident. We are not tough. The method of cutting cords, employed by many, is potentially damaging and rarely long-lasting.

**Trap 6:** Blame others for our energy. One of the biggest challenges for empaths has been discerning where our feelings begin and another person's end. As a result, we may blame others for our own energy. However, once an empath knows and grasps that we feel the energy of others, we may better understand the need to scan our own energy to ascertain what belongs to us. This scanning helps us to take responsibility for our energy. The time is here for us to check ourselves before we check others. This is minding our own energy. Using the Energy Sensing exercise in chapter 1 helps us sense energy in general. The Empath Energy Scan at the end of this chapter helps us to learn to distinguish our energy from other energy. These exercises keep us from falling into this trap.

Falling into any or all of the traps ultimately leads traditional empaths into a feeling of *can't*. Rather than seeing the many possibilities this life has to offer, we instead manage our life, and our energy, with a list of the things we cannot do, the places we cannot go, and the people we cannot see. The "can't" mentality is a concept we explore further in the next chapter.

Indeed, embracing our empathy is not an easy undertaking. It requires training and courage. It is time to stop hiding, blaming others for unwanted energy, and cutting cords. Instead, it is time we put on our superhero capes of compassion to help ourselves and thereby The Collective. Remember, we are all one, even if sometimes we don't act like it. Empaths need the training to grow in energy management because, until now, no one has stepped up to teach us. With all the information available to determine if we *are* empaths, there is very little information to help us *be* empaths.

Compassion is the calling card of many empaths. Feeling energy is natural for us empaths. As empaths, we are like sponges. Sponges have holes that soak up the liquid and cause the fibrous parts of the sponge to swell. Unless squeezed out, the fluid remains trapped in the sponge. In much the same way, empaths absorb the energy others exude. Because energy is durable, it is then confined within the empath until it is transmuted. We will learn more about transmutation in chapter 7. When we learn this process of transmutation, we can then squeeze out the sponge. We can move into a space where we embrace our empathy. However, absorbing and transmuting energy is an empath's purpose. This is not to say that empaths should not have healthy boundaries. Of course, we should! However, while boundaries are important, many current popular teachings regarding boundaries fall short of understanding the very nature of empaths. Why? Because, once again, since absorbing energy is innate in every empath, the failure to equip empaths to transmute the inevitable absorption of energy is shortsighted. The final and most crucial landing point on the Superhero's Journey is to accept that we will absorb energy, but thankfully we can also transmute the energy.

I remember going to my hometown for a baby shower held in my honor. I had attended and graduated from law school by the age of twenty-four. I got married the weekend following my law school graduation, and a year later was giving birth to my first child. I had every reason to feel confident walking into this party. Every empath reading this knows what is coming next! I went to the party and felt very self-conscious. One lady had her arms crossed the whole time; obviously, she didn't like me. Another group of friends stood in the corner gossiping; surely, they were talking about me. Later I shared that no one at the party liked me. I recall someone suggesting, in a thoughtful way, that the ladies at the party were probably not really thinking about me at all because most people are more concerned with their own issues. Now before anyone judges the advice as harsh, there is truth to the lesson. I assumed the energy was directed at me. I had some evidence for this belief. For years, if I expressed my true feelings, people often misinterpreted them as insecurity. The interpretation was incorrect because I was confident and quite accomplished. However, the empath in me, along with the uber-psychic, was unequipped. I had lived my whole life noticing and sensing everything outside of myself instead of minding my own energy.

As it turns out, one lady had lost her job. The other ladies were indeed gossiping but about who would get the solo in the church service. I did not understand that not everything I sensed was about me. In a way, empaths are reverse narcissists. Just think about it. It is important to note that empaths are often correct about what they are sensing. However, sometimes we make incorrect assumptions. Our empathy, combined with strong intuition, makes life particularly tricky at times. We sense something, and we know it as truth, yet judgment takes place. We often misinterpret the meaning of what we feel to be something about us, which then can make us insecure or too sensitive or, worst of all, paranoid. This is why it is so important to understand our ability and learn to manage it.

It helps to realize we are on a Superhero's Journey. We are learning to become Equipped Empaths, but it is a cyclical journey with three levels. The levels do not refer to our expertise or experience as empaths. We are not unequipped in our ability to feel into others. In fact, we are really darn good at that. We just don't always realize when we are doing it or what to do with the resulting energy if we do realize it. The levels are more of a representation of the absorbing Unequipped Empath evolving into the transmuting Equipped Empath. We will discuss the three levels of empaths, as demonstrated by the Superhero's Journey in chapter 3.

To transform and ultimately transmute the energy of others, we empaths must first learn to mind our own energy. In order to manage our own energy, we must know which energy belongs to us. Recognizing our own energy is a vital step in learning to transmute energy. Many empaths may think we picked up a vibe from someone else when, in actuality, the energy originated with us. The following is an exercise to help us sense our own energy. We should get into a routine of scanning our energy right when we wake up each morning. It is also important to scan our own energy before changes in situations or environments, such as before going into a meeting. Finally, we should perform an empath energy scan each night. It is helpful if we keep a journal of our energy scans. Consistency in scanning our energy will help us become aware of what energy belongs to us and what energy is not ours that we may need to transmute.

## *Exercise*
## Empath Energy Scan

This exercise will help you scan your energy so you can better ascertain what is your energy versus someone else's.

Close your eyes and draw your attention to your breath. Begin to slow down your breathing. Bring your awareness to your physical body. First, bring your attention to your feet. Notice any sensations in your feet. Slowly begin to scan up the rest of your physical body, taking note of any area of discomfort or anything out of the ordinary. Ask yourself, "How does my body feel right now? Do I feel energetic? Do I feel tired? Do I feel well? Do I feel sick?" If you don't feel well, draw your attention to that area of your physical body where you do not feel well. Try to describe what you are feeling. Become aware of your physical energy so that you will know what is yours when you are around other energy.

Now bring your awareness to your mental body. What are you thinking about? Ask yourself, "What is on my mind right now?" Perhaps you are thinking of all the things you want to accomplish today. Perhaps it is a friend who hurt your feelings. Perhaps it is a car in the shop. Let whatever thoughts are on your mind float into your awareness. It is perfectly fine to acknowledge them. They are part of your energy makeup at this moment. Become aware of how these thoughts may affect you.

Next, draw your attention to your emotional body. Your emotions get you in touch with how you are feeling right now. Become aware of your feelings of happiness, contentment, agitation, fear, anger, and any others that float into your awareness. Take note of how these feelings may affect you.

Finally, draw your attention to your spiritual body. Scan to see if you feel connected to Source. Do you feel connected to your spirit guides or energetic guardians? Do you feel connected to anything or anyone? Take note of how this connection, or lack thereof, will affect you.

Once completed, bring your hands together in the middle of your chest in a prayerlike position. Give gratitude for the information you gained from your energy scan. Ground yourself by feeling the connection from your feet to Mother Earth. You are one with her. Feel energetic roots extending from the bottoms of your feet down into the core of Mother Earth. Wrap the roots around her core and pull some energy back up through your feet and into the rest of your body. Always remember to send some of your gratitude and loving energy through your feet to Mother Earth. Now imagine a place in the cosmos such as a star or a planet. Your higher or soul self may originate from here. Visualize lassoing some of your energy around that star or planet. Give it a little tug. Now you are equally grounded between heaven and earth. When you are ready, bring your attention back into the room and your body.

Wiggle your fingers and your toes. When you are ready, slowly and gently open your eyes.

## *Exercise*
## Empath Empowerment

This exercise will help you learn to stand empowered in your energy.

Sit quietly in a safe energy space. Close your eyes. Begin to draw your attention to your breath as you calm your energy. You find yourself about to enter a room. This room is crowded, and you may feel a bit hesitant. All of the things you have told yourself, or others have told you, about being an empath may come rushing into your mind. Take a moment to feel some of those fears. You may feel overwhelmed by the crowd. You might feel there is energy you don't want to take on because you label it as negative. You may feel concerned about what the group will think about you. Or perhaps you are afraid someone will drain your energy.

Take another deep breath and step away from the door into a quiet space. Begin to remind yourself that you are in charge of your own energy. You know you need to mind your own energy before you can mind other people's energy. Just check in with yourself. How do you feel? Note anything that belongs to you. Recognize it as your energy. Tell yourself you can transmute it if you desire because you are in charge of it. But acknowledge that it is yours. Next, remind yourself that you are one of the chosen ones to help transmute energy on this earthly mission. Just because you are an empath does not mean you are meant to be miserable. You have a high calling and a unique purpose. You are a superhero for this world at this very moment in time. Being a superhero of energy is a very high calling. But you are exactly what the world needs. It is no time for you to hide. It is time for you to step into your purpose. So, put on your cape of compassion and get busy.

Now go back to the room. Lift your head and hold yourself up tall. You will in no way be bothered by anything in this room. Remember to tell yourself you are in charge of your energy and can also manage the energy by transmutation. Walk into the room as a superhero. Decide if you are ready to transmute energy. Eventually, with lots of practice, you will be able to do so. For now, just tell yourself you have the power to change the form of energy. Remember, you already are absorbing energy. You just need to practice the next step of transmuting energy. You are the brave one. You are the compassionate one. You are the one to help this world in need. You are empowered to change not only this room but the world.

Stay in the room as long as you would like. When you are ready to leave, walk out of the room, stating, "I transmute this energy with ease and grace." Use this energy to revitalize yourself because you will have more work to do. You are a victim no more. Own your power!

Once completed, bring your hands together in the middle of your chest in a prayerlike position. Give gratitude for your empowerment. Ground yourself by feeling the connection from your feet to Mother Earth. You are one with her. Feel energetic roots extending from the bottoms of your feet down into the core of Mother Earth. Wrap the roots around her core and pull some energy back up through your feet and into the rest of your body. Always remember to send some of your gratitude and loving energy through your feet to Mother Earth. Now imagine a place in the cosmos such as a star or a planet. Your higher or soul self may originate from here. Visualize lassoing some of your energy around that star or planet. Give it a little tug. Now you are equally grounded between heaven and earth. When you are ready, bring your attention back into the room and your body. Wiggle your fingers and your toes. When you are ready, slowly and gently open your eyes.

*Chapter Three*

# The Superhero's Journey
## *From Unequipped Empath to Equipped Empath*

As we grow in our understanding of our purpose as empaths, we will open up to becoming equipped in our empathy. We will no longer view it as a curse but as a superpower. Once we understand our call to adventure, we are beginning our version of the hero's journey.[4] Many of us are familiar with Joseph Campbell's hero's journey introduced in his book *The Hero with a Thousand Faces*. The hero's journey is a metaphor for the passage of transmutation all heroes go through. There are three primary levels of the journey. In this book, we will follow the Superhero's Journey through the three levels empaths traverse. For our purposes, these levels will include Unequipped Empath, Empath in Training, and Equipped Empath. These levels will help us understand how to progress from absorbing energy to ultimately transmuting energy.

---

4.  Joseph Campbell, *The Hero with a Thousand Faces* (New York: Pantheon Books, 1949), n.p.

These levels are in no way meant to imply that some empaths are better than others. We are just at different stages in managing our energy. Even as we progress, our energy management may change from day to day, moment to moment, or situation to situation. Let's take a look at these levels in more detail.

## Unequipped Empaths (Level One—Absorb)

The Unequipped Empath is at the beginning of the journey. At level one, empaths absorb energy. This is the part of the journey where we empaths may show resistance in our call to adventure. We have received little to no instruction regarding how to handle our superhero calling. We may resist it or just not understand it. Typically, at this point in the journey some type of spiritual aid or guide is available to help us; however, many of us are unaware of the assistance available at this level.

Because of our lack of or inadequate training in energy management, Unequipped Empaths are the most prevalent. We are likely enabled by prior teachings to blame many things on our empathy. Sadly, this all may be true because we have not been given, or are not utilizing, tools or sidekicks to deflect the energy. We will learn about tools to protect and deflect in chapter 4 and more advanced tools and sidekicks in part two of this book.

We may see ourselves in some or all of the following scenarios of Unequipped Empaths. Notice the prevalence of the words *I can't*.

1. I am overwhelmed by other people and at events. I often cancel or leave early. I take on the burdens of others, leaving me drained or sick after such events, which often causes me to go into hiding for days afterward. I just can't deal with it all.

2. I can't watch or read anything sad or violent because it just makes me too upset.

3. I care for others, sometimes at the expense of caring for myself. People make fun of me for caring too much. I can't get over people making fun of me for caring too much, which makes me sad or mad.

4. I have gone through traumatic events and now feel I can't be around anything that reminds me of what happened.

5. I assume others are talking about me behind my back. Also, if they seem aloof, distant, or dismissive, I take it personally and can't seem to shake it.

6. When I go to an event, I often leave worried if I said or did the wrong thing. I mentally reenact it for days and can't stop ruminating.

7. I often ask friends if they are mad at me and apologize when I have done nothing wrong. I can't accept their answer when they tell me everything is fine.

8. I can't deal with my emotions. I use sleep, alcohol, food, drugs, self-sabotaging, or other addictive behaviors to avoid my feelings.

9. I regularly dim my light to let others shine to make myself less of a perceived target. I will even stay quiet when I am knowledgeable on matters where others want the notoriety. I can't handle being hurt by anyone else.

10. I always seem to have a few people in my life whose approval I crave at a detriment to myself, but I can't do without them.

## Empaths in Training (Level Two—Deflect)

Now the Empath in Training is at the center of the journey. At level two, empaths begin to realize that not only do we absorb energy, we can deflect the energy. While we may understand we absorb energy, we might not know what to do with it yet. This is when we go into training to become superheroes instead of always hiding. This is the beginning of our transmutation. We will often have a mentor at this level. These are our superhero sidekicks. We may have many tools and sidekicks, depending on the challenges and temptations we face. There are times during this level that we may have great revelations, or we may fall into what feels like an abyss because we are absorbing energy and using defensive measures but are yet to transmute energy.

Learning to deflect and protect against energy is absolutely vital for empaths in training, and indeed everyone. At this level, we are training to utilize the newly discovered arsenal of tools at our disposal such as bubbles, eggs, mirrors, shields, and walls to protect against unwanted energy until we learn the ultimate magic of transmutation. The recognition that most empaths need more training is not a condemnation of the Empath in Training. If anything, most will be grateful for the opportunity to become Equipped Empaths. However, at this level, we are in the process of learning that despite our best efforts to deflect energy, we still absorb it. Why? Because empaths are wired to absorb energy. Frustration may set in because all of the advice, including cord cutting, has not worked. This realization opens us up to the next level to become Equipped Empaths, where we will learn to transmute the absorbed energy.

We may see ourselves in some or all of the following scenarios of empaths in training. Notice the instances where *I can't* has been replaced by *I choose*.

1. I am overwhelmed around other people and at events. Instead of canceling or leaving early, I choose to use tools of protection. This will help protect me from taking on the burdens of others.

2. If I watch or read anything sad or violent, it is my choice, and I choose to use tools of protection around myself and the television or computer.

3. I am learning it is fine to put myself first and care for myself. I also may choose to still care for and show love and kindness to people that others think don't deserve it. My tools of protection will help me not care as much what others think about my choices.

4. I have gone through traumatic events. If I happen to be around anything that reminds me of what happened, I will choose to use my tools of protection.

5. Even if I still tend to assume others are talking about me behind my back, I realize I am in training to overcome these assumptions. Also, if people seem aloof, distant, or dismissive, I am beginning to choose not to take it personally and use my tools of protection to help me.

6. Before I go to an event, I choose to use my tools of protection. This helps me begin to stop mentally reenacting it for days and stop ruminating.

7. Even if I still feel insecure at times, I choose to take people at their word and accept their answer when they tell me everything is fine.

8. I realize I am an emotional being. I am happy that I am sensitive. I choose tools of protection to guard my feelings.

9. I choose to allow myself to be seen and heard. I know my accomplishments don't take away from someone else's self-worth.

10. I choose who to have in my life and use boundaries when needed.

## Equipped Empaths (Level Three—Transmute)

Finally, the Equipped Empath is at the end of the Superhero's Journey. At level three, empaths are finally transmuting energy. The empath has fully transformed into a superhero with not only an arsenal of defensive tools, but has also learned to offensively handle energy through transmutation.

As we evolve from Unequipped Empath to Empath in Training, we have many tools at our disposal to help protect and guard us against unwanted energy. At level three, we will become less reliant on our tools or sidekicks for assistance. We will become the masters of our energy and transmute absorbed energy.

Those of us that are utilizing tools to mind our energy and to transmute the energy of ourselves and others when necessary see our empathic ability as a gift needed to help a hurting world. We understand the oneness of all, and we heal cords that connect us to others instead of futilely attempting to sever ties to which we are forever energetically bound. We will learn to transmute energy in chapter 7. The point of *The Magic of Connection* is that once we learn to transmute energy, we have evolved out of the level one and level two scenarios. We have the power to transmute whatever energy we choose. We know we can, and we will. We are superheroes with compassion as our capes.

### *Exercise*
### Where Am I on My Superhero's Journey? (Take One)

The following exercise will help you assess where you are on your Superhero's Journey. A copy of this assessment is also located in chapter 17, so you can reevaluate it at that time.

Assess where you are on your Superhero's Journey by rating the following fifteen statements. Be honest in your assessment, realizing that you never remain in the same place on your journey. The journey is cyclical. While you might be quite evolved in some parts of your journey, you might need improvement in other areas. Transmutation takes practice and diligence. Return to this self-assessment any time you want to assess your energy. It also helps to journal regarding opportunities for improvement and what situations might trigger regression.

(Scoring: Scale from 1-5. Never = 1, Seldom = 2, Sometimes = 3, Often = 4, Always = 5)

1. I am overwhelmed in social situations.
2. I have anxiety, and it keeps me from doing things.
3. I put others ahead of myself to my detriment.
4. I self-sabotage.
5. I am affected by people's energy.
6. I take on the burdens of others.
7. I can't watch or read anything violent.
8. I care for others at the expense of myself.
9. I can't be around anything that triggers past traumatic events.
10. I worry what other people think of me.
11. I mentally replay things I have said or done.
12. I dim my light instead of allowing myself to shine.
13. I avoid confrontation.
14. I feel drained after events.
15. I let energy affect me.

Scoring Results: Tally your total score. If you scored 15 to 30, you are currently operating at the Equipped Empath level. If you scored 31 to 52, you are currently operating at the Empath in Training level. If you scored 53 to 75, you are currently operating at the Unequipped Empath level. Remember, our journey is not linear; it is cyclical. We are multidimensional beings. No level is better or worse than the other. Just let it guide you, not label you. Allow yourself to be in the energy of the journey.

*Chapter Four*

# Bubbles and Mirrors and Eggs...Oh My
## *Protection and Deflection*

For all the talk we hear of raising our vibration and good vibes, it seems we struggle more with what has become a catchall term: *negativity*. Negativity, or a form thereof, is a buzzword these days. It represents anything and everyone that we decide is something we don't like. We have embraced a culture of confrontation avoidance. All too often, we say or hear phrases such as *I just can't deal with that negative energy. There is a low vibration in that house. My office is toxic.* A coworker may seem in an irritable mood or a great mood; they are still the same person but presenting their energy in varying forms. We are equipping ourselves in energy management once we begin to accept this and stop labeling the energy. A vital part of learning to become an Equipped Empath is to learn this energy management. For example, we will not let this coworker bother us as much. We will merely take a step back and realize their energy has a different vibration. It probably has nothing to do with us. This bystander observation is the beginning phase of learning to transmute or change energy.

We may find ourselves in a cycle of labeling vibrational energy instead of just being in the energy. This energy is more often labeled as unfavorable because we lean toward a negativity bias. We are more likely to remember a criticism than a compliment. With all the talk of positive thinking, many still are inclined to negativism. This bent toward a negativity bias seems ironic because we genuinely crave positivity, but all too often, the pain outweighs the joy. Nevertheless, it is clear that high vibration is associated with labels of happiness, laughter, compassion, love, serenity, and bliss. Low vibration is related to labels of sadness, crying, anger, hatred, depression, anxiety, and stress.

It is essential to realize that there is a time for negative emotions. Categorizing emotions such as anger or frustration as low vibration results in many wanting to bypass experiencing necessary, although painful feelings. This categorization of emotions, and any subsequent desire to avoid them, leads to even more so-called lower vibration feelings such as fear, shame, and guilt. It is unhealthy to avoid these emotions entirely. Many people stuff these feelings only to develop worse symptoms from denial. It is imperative that we realize we will have these feelings and that they need acknowledgment. Sometimes we need to lean into things, situations, and emotions that don't feel great. If not, we will, perhaps unintentionally, perpetuate the cycle of so-called negativity or low vibration. We are always fluctuating between high and low frequencies. Perhaps the issue is not so much in the labeling of the energy, but the judgment associated with the label. For example, rose quartz is conventionally known as a stone of unconditional love; ironically enough, however, it is a low vibration crystal. Therefore, this frequency fluctuation is natural and should not receive judgment.

Experiencing things at our own pace is part of the earthly experience. This is experiencing the Law of Duality. While a label may be assigned to the energy, the judgment of the energy is problematic. Remember the radio channels we spoke of earlier? Just as an aside, it is interesting to note that many times when we are sad, we find ourselves listening to sad songs. Country western music is heart-wrenching at times, yet it is cathartic on some level. Leaning into those emotions, instead of avoiding them, is sometimes the very thing that leads to an emotional breakthrough instead of a nervous breakdown.

Just like there are many lists to determine if you are an empath, there are many lists to determine if you are high or low vibration. The very notion that someone self-appoints themselves the judge of vibration shows they may not understand the Law of Vibration and the Law of Relativity. As we better understand these laws, we will begin to lose judgment.

As an Empath in Training, we will, at times, lean into negativity and need our tools of protection. I remember road trips as a child. My friend and I would sit in the backseat. Inevitably, about ten minutes into the trip, we would draw an imaginary line down the middle of the seat. Neither of us was to cross that boundary line. Many arguments ensued about the technical placement of the line. I'm pretty sure I was crossing the line on many occasions. But the fact that we had the established boundary eventually led to some feeling of having our own energetic space.

The idea of energetic boundaries such as bubbles, eggs, and shields provides a starting point to energy management. There are many suggested forms of energy protection available to us. These include, but are not limited to, eggs, bubbles, zip-ups, and violet, golden, or even white light. While these protection methods may prove useful in shielding us from someone else's allegedly lousy energy, we still encounter so-called negative energy.

In using these tools of protection, it is vital to understand that we all have an energy field called an auric field that surrounds our bodies. Everything, from plants to crystals, has its own aura. We are continually bumping auras with something or someone. Our auras consist of seven different layers. The seven auric layers connect to the seven energy fields in our bodies called chakras. The first layer of our auric field is known as the etheric layer. This layer is closest to and represents our physical body. This etheric layer connects to the root chakra, which is the energetic field related to our physical needs and survival instincts. Interestingly, the etheric body is the easiest to see with the naked eye.

The second layer of our auric field is our emotional body. This layer represents our feelings and emotions and connects to our sacral chakra. Our sacral chakra is the energetic field related to pleasure, creativity, and passion. The third layer of our auric field is our mental body. The mental body represents our thoughts, mind, and cognition. It connects to our solar plexus, which is our power center of self-worth. The fourth layer of our auric field is our astral layer. This layer is where we often form our astral cords with others and connects to the heart chakra. The heart chakra is the energetic center of love, compassion, and empathy.

The fifth layer of our auric field is our etheric template. The etheric template represents and includes the entire blueprint for the physical plane, including our personality, identity, and energy. The etheric template connects to our throat chakra, the energy center for speaking our truth, feeling heard, and listening. The sixth layer is our celestial body. The celestial body represents our connection to Source and other beings. It has a stable vibration associated with unconditional love and a feeling of oneness. The celestial body connects to the brow chakra or third eye, which is our energetic center of intuition and discernment. The seventh layer is the ketheric template. It is furthest away from the physical body. It represents oneness with All and vibrates at the highest frequency. It connects to the crown chakra, which is our energetic center of spirituality and enlightenment.

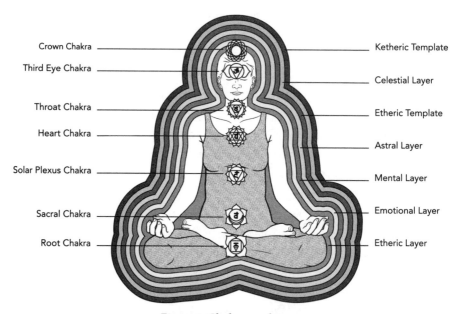

*Figure 1: Chakras and Aura*

Do we need bubbles, shields, and eggs to protect our auric fields? The answer, in our earliest stages of energy management, is absolutely yes! As an Unequipped Empath, we absorb energy sometimes without even being aware of it. As we move into Empath in Training on our Superhero's Journey, we learn we need to deflect the energy we are prone to absorb until we learn to transmute it. This is why we need tools at this stage. As noted earlier, we are always bumping into the auric fields of someone or something. It never hurts to have extra protection given all the bumping auras. Much like wearing a helmet, it will still hurt if we fall off our bike and bump our head, but wearing the helmet protects from more severe damage. However, please know that we will be exposed to other related energy many times during the full course of our days. The tools we use will not insulate us entirely; they will just help protect us from other energy we encounter. Later we still may use defensive tools periodically, but we will begin to transmute the energy more frequently.

## Bubble of Protection

Bubbles of protection are a popular form of energy protection. These are helpful in any type of everyday situation where we may feel the energy of others, yet we don't necessarily feel a direct attack by them. A bubble of protection is easy to envision at any time of day or night. When beginning, it is best to visualize the bubble first thing in the morning. We simply visualize a clear bubble extending out from around our physical bodies in every direction. Our energy may go out to others if we desire.

Further, the energy of others will not penetrate the bubble. If we so choose, we can purposefully allow the vibes of others to reach us. For this protection method to indeed be effective, a lot of visualization and intention setting is involved. The drawback to this tool in our superhero arsenal is that if we use it all the time, we may start to feel isolated and cut off from the world. We will learn later that, with practice, transmuting energy may take much less effort and will allow us to interact with those around us fully.

## Egg of Protection

The egg is, in many ways, similar to the bubble. This form of energy protection is helpful in any type of everyday situation where we may feel the energy of others, yet we don't necessarily feel a direct attack. The egg might serve as protection when we feel anxious or we are in large crowds. With the egg, we encapsulate either our body or our entire auric fields. This total encapsulation means that, in some instances, the egg may go up to twenty feet from our auric fields. The broad area the egg may cover is intriguing because we clearly will be intermingling with the auric fields or eggs of protection of others.

Like the bubble, for the process of protection to be effective, we must use visualization and intention setting. The drawback to this tool in our superhero arsenal is that if we use it all the time, we may start to feel isolated and cut off from the world. We also must realize that our security will overlap with other auric fields. We will learn later that, with practice, transmuting energy may take much less effort and will allow us to interact with those around us fully.

## Shield or Armor of Protection

Shields or armor are ways to deflect unwanted energy. This type of protection is useful when we feel we are going into an emotional war zone. It will help us feel empowered and confident. A drawback of this method of protection is it may prevent us from ever dealing with the issue. It is yet another form of avoidance. Avoiding the very problems and people that we came to the earth to learn from is often illogical. We need to face many of these issues and transmute the energy; however, the shield and armor may help us until we equip ourselves to confront the problems and convert the energy.

## Mirrors

Imagining mirrors around us like a disco ball will help us reflect the energy back to the sender. Mirrors are suitable if we are in crowded spaces or feel more personally attacked and have not learned to transmute large amounts of energy. Similar to the shield, the drawback of this tool of protection is that it may eventually prevent us from growing in and managing our energy. We will learn later that, with practice, transmuting energy may take much less effort and will allow us to interact with those around us fully.

## Invisibility Cloak or Jumpsuit

If we want to go unnoticed when around others, we can visualize zipping ourselves up in a transparent cloak or jumpsuit from head to toe. We will be able to operate normally energetically, but others will not be able to interact with us. It will be as if we are not there, almost like a fly on the wall. This tool is useful in situations when we want to focus on the task and not be bothered by other energy. It is especially helpful for children or the vulnerable. An invisibility cloak or suit is the ultimate form of hiding from other energy. The drawback to this tool is that if we overuse it, we may begin to feel isolated and even as if we don't exist. Eventually, we will become adept at transmuting energy and may choose to use it less often.

## Wall of Protection

A wall of protection is a barrier between us and other energy, which is very difficult to penetrate. It is ideal for times when we feel incredibly vulnerable, fearful, fragile, or under attack. It serves to protect us until we are strong enough and have called in sidekicks to help us. The drawback with walls of protection is we often are placing ourselves in prisons of our own making because we find it harder and harder to ever break through the walls. We also may realize we have walled ourselves in with energy, which we originally blame on someone else only to realize is our own. As we evolve in our energy management, we will isolate and wall off less and less. We will no longer buy into the lie that we cannot handle any so-called negativity.

As an Empath in Training, these tools of protection allow us to replace many of our *can't* paradigms with *choose* paradigms. There is caution necessary in using these tools. We often believe they need to grow in strength. Additionally, over the time of relying on bubbles, eggs, shields, and armor, we may have never learned to interact with other energy. We have yet to learn to transmute energy. Failure to equip ourselves for energy management is tragic because it is a self-fulfilling prophecy. We are so afraid of negative energy that our temporary measures of protection ultimately disempower us.

A lot, if not most, of our energy issues come from within us. We become upset and create negative thought-forms and find ourselves in a loop of negativity. We look for ways to block outside energy without first clearing our own. What happens when we put a shield around ourselves? We simply wall in our own unhandled negativity. We are so quick to blame other sources that we forget to mind our own energy.

Just as energy never goes away but merely changes form, such is the case with our thoughts. Our thoughts linger and eventually evolve into thought-forms. In the extreme, thought-forms can be powerful and even scary. After my divorce from my husband of twenty-six years, he sued me to modify our initial agreement. I was scared and angry. We are both trial attorneys, and I knew how we tried cases. A courthouse bloodbath was about to ensue. As time went on, I became more and more scared and angry. A spiritual mentor asked me if I had been lighting candles in my home. Of course, she didn't mean pumpkin spice candles for the kitchen. She meant candles of intention. I admitted I had lit a few candles and put herbs in them. Well, it was probably about eight different candles. Candles lined my kitchen counter. The candles covered the court case, my ex, his girlfriend, the judge, money, communication, and many more subjects. Did I know how to set an intention with candles? Yes. Did I know what color candle to use? Yes. Did I know what types of herbs to use? Yes. But none of that mattered when I did not mind my energy. I was furious and fearful, and that energy was intense. My mentor had seen, in her third eye, a thought-form that I had created. It was hanging out in my home, and it was a thought-form some might label as a demon. Through the power of my emotions, I created an entity. Eventually, I did a thorough, energetic clearing of my home, and the thought-form went on its way. I often think of the power of my anger and fear. I also think of the fact that the thought-form never really went away. It just left my home. I did not transmute or change the energy. I also did not change it in my cord of connection for several years. I bubbled, I egged, I cleared, I saged, I shielded, I walled. I even tried to cut cords. But I fell short of the most important aspect of energy management. I failed to transmute the energy.

Just as we feed energy to thought-forms, thereby enhancing their growth, we often strengthen energetic ties by giving them attention. This strengthening includes cutting cords over and over again. By the very nature of providing the cords more energy by trying to sever them, we are doing the exact opposite of what we are trying to accomplish. Eventually, we will learn to perceive energy the way energy sees energy. There will be no label. The intention behind the energy will fade away, and only the energy will remain. This type of transmutation is a very advanced technique that requires much focused practice.

Many of us have defense mechanisms that work most of our lives. However, when these defense mechanisms no longer work for us, we decompensate. Our personality may change; we may experience uncontrollable rage;

we may experience devastating despair or any other extreme emotion. We have lost our defense mechanisms. In the same way, bubbles and mirrors and eggs may work for some time, but eventually, they fail us. Oh my!

*Exercise*
## Bubble of Protection

This exercise is useful for all situations, whether you think you need protection or not.

Sit quietly in a safe space. Close your eyes. Begin to draw your attention to your breath as you calm your energy. Begin to visualize a clear bubble surrounding your whole person. Expand the bubble away from your body. With time and practice, you will know how far or close to keep your bubble. You feel comfortable in your bubble. You can do all the things you usually do. Your energy and light can go out to others. Set the intention that the bubble will not allow in any energy that does not serve your best and highest good. Trust that your higher self, that part of yourself that is egoless, will know what you should be protected from. Yet, realize that at some point, the bubble will become less critical. Your ability to transmute the energy instead of protecting yourself from it grows stronger each day.

Once completed, bring your hands together at your heart chakra in a prayerlike position. Give gratitude for your bubble of protection. Ground yourself by feeling the connection from your feet to Mother Earth. You are one with her. Feel energetic roots extending from the bottoms of your feet down into the core of Mother Earth. Wrap the roots around her core and pull some energy back up through your feet and into the rest of your body. Always remember to send some of your gratitude and loving energy through your feet to Mother Earth. Now imagine a place in the cosmos such as a star or a planet. Your higher or soul self may originate from here. Visualize lassoing some of your energy around that star or planet. Give it a little tug. Now you are equally grounded between heaven and earth. When you are ready, bring your attention back into the room and your body. Wiggle your fingers and your toes. When you are ready, slowly and gently open your eyes.

## *Exercise*
## Egg of Protection

This exercise is helpful when you feel incredibly anxious or are in large crowds.

Sit quietly in a safe space. Close your eyes. Begin to draw your attention to your breath as you calm your energy. Begin to visualize an egg surrounding your whole person or even your entire auric field. The egg may extend up to twenty feet away from your body. With time and practice, you will know how far or close to keep your egg. You feel comfortable in your egg. It feels similar to lying under a weighted blanket. You can do all the things you usually do. Your energy and light can go out to others. You may realize, as you become more aware of energy, that your egg is in the auric fields of other beings. Set the intention that the egg will not allow in any energy that does not serve your best and highest good. Trust that your higher self, that part of yourself that is egoless, will know when you need protection. Yet realize that at some point, the egg will become less important as you embrace your ability to transmute the energy instead of protecting yourself from it.

Once completed, bring your hands together at your heart chakra in a prayerlike position. Give gratitude for your egg of protection. Ground yourself by feeling the connection from your feet to Mother Earth. You are one with her. Feel energetic roots extending from the bottoms of your feet down into the core of Mother Earth. Wrap the roots around Her core and pull some energy back up through your feet and into the rest of your body. Always remember to send some of your gratitude and loving energy through your feet to Mother Earth. Now imagine a place in the cosmos such as a star or a planet. Your higher or soul self may originate from here. Visualize lassoing some of your energy around that star or planet. Give it a little tug. Now you are equally grounded between heaven and earth. When you are ready, bring your attention back into the room and your body. Wiggle your fingers and your toes. When you are ready, slowly and gently open your eyes.

## *Exercise*
## Shield or Armor of Protection

This exercise is helpful when you feel you are under attack.

Sit quietly in a safe space. Close your eyes. Begin to draw your attention to your breath as you calm your energy. If you need, take more time to calm your energy. Begin to visualize yourself carrying a shield, wearing armor, or both. The shield and armor are durable and protect any area where you feel attacked. You feel comfortable in your armor and adept with your shield. You are ready for any emotional battle that comes your way. Your energy and light can go out to others. Set the intention that the shield and armor will not allow in any energy that does not serve your best and highest good. Trust that your higher self, that part of yourself that is egoless, will know what needs protection. Realize that at some point, the shield and armor will become less important as you embrace your ability to transmute the energy instead of protecting yourself from it.

Once completed, bring your hands together at your heart chakra in a prayerlike position. Give gratitude for your shield or armor of protection. Ground yourself by feeling the connection from your feet to Mother Earth. You are one with her. Feel energetic roots extending from the bottoms of your feet down into the core of Mother Earth. Wrap the roots around her core and pull some energy back up through your feet and into the rest of your body. Always remember to send some of your gratitude and loving energy through your feet to Mother Earth. Now imagine a place in the cosmos such as a star or a planet. Your higher or soul self may originate from here. Visualize lasso-ing some of your energy around that star or planet. Give it a little tug. Now you are equally grounded between heaven and earth. When you are ready, bring your attention back into the room and your body. Wiggle your fingers and your toes. When you are ready, slowly and gently open your eyes.

*Exercise*
## Mirrors

This exercise is useful when you feel attacked by an individual or a group of people.

Sit quietly in a safe space. Close your eyes. Begin to draw your attention to your breath as you calm your energy. If you need, take more time to calm your energy. This type of work is often necessary when you are quite upset with someone or a group of people. Begin to visualize yourself inside a disco ball of mirrors. The ball spins, and the mirrors cast reflections all around the space. The mirrors begin to send any energy directed your way back to the sender. You are ready for any energy that comes your way. Your energy and light can go out to others. Set the intention that the bubble of mirrors will return to the sender any energy that does not serve your best and highest good. Trust that your higher self, that part of yourself that is egoless, will know what energy is not good for you. Realize that at some point, the bubble of mirrors will become less important as you embrace your ability to transmute the energy instead of protecting yourself from it.

Once completed, bring your hands together at your heart chakra in a prayerlike position. Give gratitude for your mirrors. Ground yourself by feeling the connection from your feet to Mother Earth. You are one with her. Feel energetic roots extending from the bottoms of your feet down into the core of Mother Earth. Wrap the roots around her core and pull some energy back up through your feet and into the rest of your body. Always remember to send some of your gratitude and loving energy through your feet to Mother Earth. Now imagine a place in the cosmos such as a star or a planet. Your higher or soul self may originate from here. Visualize lassoing some of your energy around that star or planet. Give it a little tug. Now you are equally grounded between heaven and earth. When you are ready, bring your attention back into the room and your body. Wiggle your fingers and your toes. When you are ready, slowly and gently open your eyes.

### *Exercise*
### Invisibility Cloak or Jumpsuit

This exercise is useful when you want to be alone, yet you still have to interact with others.

Sit quietly in a safe space. Close your eyes. Begin to draw your attention to your breath as you calm your energy. You feel a great need to hide for a while. Begin to visualize zipping yourself up from head to toe in a see-through cloak or jumpsuit. You can move around totally unnoticed energetically. You can operate normally. You can be a fly on the wall. Your energy and light can go out to others. Set the intention that the invisibility cloak or jumpsuit will keep you hidden from any energy that seeks to find you—the energy that does not serve your best and highest good. Trust that your higher self, that part of yourself that is egoless, will know what energy does not help you. Realize that at some point, the invisibility cloak or jumpsuit will become less important as you embrace your ability to transmute the energy instead of hiding from it.

Once completed, bring your hands together at your heart chakra in a prayerlike position. Give gratitude for your jumpsuit or invisibility cloak of protection. Ground yourself by feeling the connection from your feet to Mother Earth. You are one with her. Feel energetic roots extending from the bottoms of your feet down into the core of Mother Earth. Wrap the roots around her core and pull some energy back up through your feet and into the rest of your body. Always remember to send some of your gratitude and loving energy through your feet to Mother Earth. Now imagine a place in the cosmos such as a star or a planet. Your higher or soul self may originate from here. Visualize lassoing some of your energy around that star or planet. Give it a little tug. Now you are equally grounded between heaven and earth. When you are ready, bring your attention back into the room and your body. Wiggle your fingers and your toes. When you are ready, slowly and gently open your eyes.

*Exercise*
## Wall of Protection

This exercise is useful when you feel like everyone and everything is against you. It is also useful when you are feeling fragile, fearful, or hopeless.

Sit quietly in a safe space. Close your eyes. Begin to draw your attention to your breath as you calm your energy. If you need, take more time to calm your energy. This type of work is often helpful when you are feeling very defensive and perhaps hopeless. Begin to visualize yourself behind a strong wall. The wall is tall and goes for as far as you can see. You feel protected from any energy that comes your way. You can try to extend your energy and light beyond the wall, but you probably do not want to do so or do not have the strength. Set your intention to mind your own energy because—get this—you have walled yourself off with that energy. Set the intention that the wall will protect you from any energy that does not serve your best and highest good. Trust that your higher self, that part of yourself that is egoless, will know what does not serve your highest and best good. Realize that at some point, the wall might become a prison of your own making. Rest assured, it will become less important as you embrace your ability to transmute the energy instead of protecting yourself from it.

Once completed, bring your hands together in the middle of your chest in a prayerlike position. Give gratitude for your wall of protection. Ground yourself by feeling the connection from your feet to Mother Earth. You are one with her. Feel energetic roots extending from the bottoms of your feet down into the core of Mother Earth. Wrap the roots around her core and pull some energy back up through your feet and into the rest of your body. Always remember to send some of your gratitude and loving energy through your feet to Mother Earth. Now imagine a place in the cosmos such as a star or a planet. Your higher or soul self may originate from here. Visualize lassoing some of your energy around that star or planet. Give it a little tug. Now you are equally grounded between heaven and earth. When you are ready, bring your attention back into the room and your body. Wiggle your fingers and your toes. When you are ready, slowly and gently open your eyes.

# Chapter Five

# Every Encounter Is a Cord Encounter
## *The Cords We Weave*

A cord is an energetic connection. Cords are also known as ties, strings, hooks, jumper cables, and strands. Many go to great lengths to differentiate between the names given to connections. For example, drains or hooks often receive a more dramatic characterization than cords. A drain is often described as a type of attachment that depletes us of our energy, often without us realizing why. It is often said that a needy friend who wears us out may unintentionally become a drain. A hook may carry a more insidious implication in that perhaps someone has purposefully hooked a malevolent cord in us. As we become more and more aware of our own energy, we will be much more prepared to deal with other energy. So, while the labels bear noting, it is not that important for us to spend a lot of time worrying over them.

Are there those who will attempt to intentionally leech onto us and drain us of our life force or energy if they sense our light? Absolutely. They do this by firing up a cord of connection. Should we utilize some defensive measures?

Yes. However, it is more important for us to be aware of our own energy and how it subsequently interacts with the energy of others. This way, we will be prepared if we encounter such a psychic vampire or one that drains us of our life force. Then we will not only be prepared defensively but also ready to transform any energy malevolently thrown at us. But in general, the minute we begin to label what everyone else has done to us, we have stepped out of minding our energy and back into giving our power to others.

There are many more critical repeated misconceptions, unquestioned teachings, and unsupervised healings regarding the concept of cords. One of the biggest fallacies regarding cords is that they only run between certain people. Many opine that the cords are between people to whom we have some singular sort of connection. This belief is a misleading description of energetic cords. In actuality, they run between all of us because we are all connected and all one. Cords run between anything that is energy. Because everything is energy, cords also connect us to everything.

Furthermore, everything connects through cords. The fact that everything connects through these strands of energy is hard for us to fathom in our finite minds. But everything and everyone is literally bound together by energetic strands. Imagine the etheric connection as multiple strands of Christmas lights connecting and lighting up an entire city. Many of the cords may go unnoticed for our entire lifetime. They may lie dormant, just like lights that are never turned on, but they are still there. It is important to know we have an infinite number of ties attaching us to All That Is. This unlimited number of cords is six degrees of separation made simple. Simply put, there is no separation. There is merely an illusion of individuality. Yes, we are unique energy bodies, but we are all corded together in one way or another.

Another frequent assumption is that cords are always negative. We hear this erroneous assumption of negativity over and over again. Let's set the record straight. Cords are energy-filled ties between all of us. They can be perceived as positive, negative, neutral, and everything in between. The connections vary with every person, situation, or energy. The strength of the bond may vary based on circumstances, but there is a bond in every encounter. The strength of the connection depends on the attention we give it. For instance, we are corded with someone on the other side of the world that we have never met or considered. We can think of that cord as neutral, dormant, or not activated. Remember, it is less important what we call it than how we visualize and describe it. Imagine a person that passes us on the street. An energetic union exists between that person and us. The strength of that union is affected by how the person's energy feels to us. If we pass on the street, seemingly unaware of one another, the cord is not activated. But make no mistake, it is still there. If the person smiles at us, the cord brightens up a bit. It is activated.

On the other hand, if we have an adverse reaction such as the person frowns at us, the cord will also activate, but in a *red flag* way. Either way, the cord is there, but once attention comes to the connection, the cord will activate. It is as though the cord is turning on or firing up. In other words, it is no longer dormant. The cord may feel one way to one of the participants and another way to the other due to the Law of Relativity.

This activation, or lack thereof, also exists with buildings or houses. We may pass a building every day and think nothing of it. However, if we walk in the building, we may sense the energy of the building, and the cord will fire up. If we have a significant event occur in the building, the bond will become even stronger.

The health of the cord is also a consideration. The health of the cord is determined by the energy of both beings. For far too long, we have thought one of the beings could solely influence the health of a cord. For instance, we have assumed one end of the cord could throw energetic shade through the cord, and all we could do was protect from it and hope for the best. This concept of one-way energy with nothing but defensive mentality is faulty thinking. Not only can we play defense when needed and use protective measures, we are the superheroes needed to begin healing cords of connection. Healthy cords are those where we have love and light flowing through the cord. These cords may appear as shining, glowing, sparkling, radiating, glittering beautiful cords. Unhealthy cords are cords where lower vibrations affect them. Unhealthy cords may appear as dull, cloudy, muddy, muted, murky, shadowy, ugly cords. An exercise for visualizing cords is included at the end of this chapter.

It is interesting to note some of the most powerful connections. One such relationship is that of parents to children. An umbilical cord is a physical and magical connection between mothers and children. Yet there are also cords between fathers and children. The ties also exist between biological parents or adopted parents. What is essential is that the strength and health of the connection depend on the relationship. While at birth, the cord connects from sacral chakra to sacral chakra. Over time, a healthy, loving mother will look after her child, and the cord will often connect from heart chakra to heart chakra. It may be bright, shiny, and robust. It could be pink or green, but whatever the color, it is clear and bright. If a mother is a helicopter mom, always swooping in and rescuing the child or interfering where she should give the child wings, the cord may still have tenacious durability. However, the cord may begin to take on a muddier color. It may look more like a sturdy vine. If the mother is abusive, the cord will still have durability, but the cord may begin to look like a rope or a chain. There is still a cord connecting the two.

The bond does not need severing. The bond needs healing. This is a perfect example of the difficulty in labeling energy as positive or negative. One mother-daughter relationship may thrive with extremely close ties, while another may seem toxic and suffocating. The beings involved in the energetic cording must learn to identify the vibration flowing between the cords— between the two energetic beings. They must learn to see if this is in alignment or a state of agreement with how their higher self wants to feel. The higher self is that part of them that knows what is best for them no matter what they may want. Is this easy? No, this is not easy. It is difficult for us to become aware of our true higher calling. That part of us that knows what is best for our soul. But as we begin to get in touch with our own energy, we will become more familiar with what truly is in alignment with our energy. Then we will begin to take responsibility for our own energy instead of blaming others. Only then will we truly begin to step into the empowerment that so many have promised us.

Another powerful connection where many of us need to step into true empowerment is the connection between sexual partners. Often the reason hookups so profoundly affect us is because of cording. Even a casual hookup will activate the energetic cord between the individuals. Casual hookup cords often dig in profoundly and grab hold. Once again, the energy flowing through the cord may have different energy coming from the various sources. If two individuals have a casual hookup with *no strings attached*, one of the individuals may send very little energy through the cord. However, if the other person is more attached, there will be more energy activation. If we do consider the term "hook," a description of a cord that sinks in and attaches deeply, we might realize the irony of the phrase hookup. Sexual energy often produces strong ropes between individuals.

There are also connections between us that sometimes seem to suck the life out of us. We all have that friend who seems to be an energy vampire. Whether they realize it or not, they insert a needle into us with an intravenous bag attached. They then begin to drain away our life force. These drains, which were previously mentioned, are exhausting and often lead to depression or chronic fatigue for those drained of energy. However, an accurate understanding of energy management through *The Magic of Connection* will give us a new understanding of using the phrase *energy or psychic vampire*. While society traditionally assigns negative connotations to this phrase, the denotation "energy vampire" is someone who takes on someone else's energy.

Let us consider the friend that is bringing us down. Their constant complaining and so-called negative energy are said to drain us. As we begin to understand the appropriate transmutation of energy, we will realize that their energy is there for us to transmute to a higher vibration instead of us letting it drag us down. In this way, we become the energy vampire. Oh, I hear you now. *That is horrible!* Before judging the thought of becoming an energy vampire, many of us have already admitted, as empaths, that we absorb everyone else's energy. Well, guess what? That is an energy vampire. The distinction between the traditional usage of the phrase energy vampire versus our usage is the cognizance and intention of the taking of the energy. Up until now, many of us have just not realized our ability to wear a vampire cape of another sort—a superhero cape where we transmute the energy for The Collective's higher good. We are transmutation energy vampires.

The strength of any cord of connection depends on how much fuel the connection receives. One person may feed the relationship more than the other person. These factors make for all types of cords. Some are weak, thin, wispy cords while others are durable, thick, dense cables. Some are beautiful shiny gold or silver tinsel, while others are gray and rotten. They may even smell putrid. The health of the cord all depends on the strength of the connection and the energy that has traveled through the cord of connection.

It is critical to realize that every single encounter we have with anything or anyone has a connection. As we are more and more aware of this, we become more mindful of every energetic exchange we experience. For example, the next time we interact with someone waiting on us at a restaurant, we may think more carefully about how we are treating them. We can literally begin to transmute energy. If we try to transmute the energy while we are active in the encounter, we will not have to heal cords later. We can choose to smile and say *thank you.* We can choose to leave that person a little bit better off than when we first encountered them. Changing the course of someone's day for the better is transmutation in action. It is quite simple. Let us practice treating others the way we want to be treated. We should only transmute energy between cords to promote growth and development to help someone or something on its evolutionary path. If we frame our behavior in such a way that we will be proud to repeat how we handled it, we know we have begun to solidify healthy energy management. We are on our way to becoming energy superheroes.

*Exercise*
## Cord Visualization
This exercise will help you recognize and visualize your cords of connection.

Sit quietly in a safe space. Close your eyes. Begin to draw your attention to your breath as you calm your energy. Bring your attention to your etheric layer, which represents your physical body. Notice any sensation that feels out of the ordinary, odd, uncomfortable, or even painful. Allow this area to float into your mind. Begin to visualize the area of your physical body as if you were zooming in on that particular area. Once you have a good view, begin to look for anything that may be attached to this area, such as a cord or a tie. If you find a cord, begin to examine how it is attached and what it looks like. Is it hanging loosely as if by a thread? Is it wrapped around tightly? Is it wispy and thin? Is it strong and thick? What color is it? Does it appear new or old? Explore and examine this energetic cord for as long as you desire.

If you do not know the most immediate source of this cord, perhaps follow it with your mind to the most direct source. If this is an energetic connection that has great flow of energy from one direction to you, sit with this energy. Merely be the observer of the energy. Is there any energy flowing from you through the cord? What is the vibration of that energy? If you determine this is a connection that needs healing, begin to visualize beautiful, bright, golden light flowing from you through the cord. You can add in the bright light of healing, emerald green. Ask and intend that the vibration remains high and that you remain merely a bystander to the energy flow. Flood the cord with healing light. Imagine so much healing light going through the cord that there is no room for anything else to come through the cord back toward you unless your higher self so chooses. Your higher self is that part of you that knows your overall soul plan for all lifetimes and would only have your best interest in mind, absent any ego. Set the intention that this healing light will continue to flow through the cord and that no further action will be required of your human form. Repeat this process with each of your other auric fields (emotional, mental, astral, etheric template, celestial, and ketheric). These could be the same cords or multiple cords in various layers. Once you have repeated the process for all of your layers of energy, take a deep breath in and exhale any fatigue.

Once completed, bring your hands together in the middle of your chest in a prayerlike position. Give gratitude for locating and visualizing your cords of connection. Ground yourself by feeling the connection from your feet to Mother Earth. You are one with her. Feel energetic roots extending from the bottoms of your feet down into the core of Mother Earth. Wrap the roots around her core and pull some energy back up through your feet and into the rest of your body. Always remember to send some of your gratitude and loving energy through your feet to Mother Earth. Now imagine a place in the cosmos such as a star or a planet. Your higher or soul self may originate from here. Visualize lassoing some of your energy around that star or planet. Give it a little tug. Now you are equally grounded between heaven and earth. When you are ready, bring your attention back into the room and your body. Wiggle your fingers and your toes. When you are ready, slowly and gently open your eyes.

*Exercise*
## Recognizing Different Cord Encounters

This exercise will help you further recognize and visualize different cords of connection.

With each cord of connection, using the Cord Visualization exercise, describe how the cord looks, sounds, smells, and feels. Describe it in detail. If you can ascertain where the cord connects to you and the other energy, describe that also. This is a list to get you started. Remember, you are corded to every type of energy, and everything is energy, so there is no limit to this exercise.

- Immediate family members
- Friends
- Coworkers
- Your community
- People you pass or encounter on a daily basis
- Strangers that you encounter
- Animal companions
- Spiritual leaders
- Political leaders
- Authority figures
- Your work
- Sexual encounters
- Societal rules and mores
- Lawsuits
- Gossip
- Health
- Specific buildings
- Specific events
- Cities, Counties, States, Countries
- Mother Nature and beings associated with her

- Good and bad memories
- Trauma
- Those who have passed
- Ghosts or disincarnates
- Ancestors
- Guides

*Chapter Six*

# Knife-Happy Healers

## *Cord Cutting Does Not Work*

Those who advocate cord cutting often focus on those that are causing us some form of discomfort. The focus on distress is understandable because many people do not become aware of cords until they are in some sort of pain. Then they seek help and are eventually told to cut the tie. Rarely are the cords of positive connection discussed. It is also important to begin focusing on cords of joy, comfort, love, and compassion. When we learn to identify the healthy cords, it gives us a point of reference for healing the unhealthy cords.

The biggest misconception or antiquated belief is what we are told to do when we no longer want a connection to someone. Cutting cords is often erroneously suggested. In short, cutting cords is a process of energetically severing the cord in an attempt to stop the flow of energy between the two beings. We often see this in *meme mantras* of a hurting person on social media. The scenario goes something like this: the hurting one posts about how they no longer need someone and are cutting that person out of their life. Or, more ironically, they speak of how they are totally over someone and cut cords with them. The sad truth is screaming through the screen. If the cords are indeed cut, why do they need to post about it at all? Why are they still talking about it? Did the cord cutting accomplish the intended goal? Of course not. It is painfully evident to everyone.

Once again, the problem with this cutting process is we are all one. We are connected. Therefore, we can try to cut cords, and it may even seem to work temporarily, but eventually, we feel the attachment once again. Cutting cords is doomed by definition because we are all one and all connected.

Let's consider the aspen tree. One aspen tree is a sprout of a sprawling network of roots that lie underground. Each tree in this extensive network is a genetic replica of the others, hence a group of aspen trees is referred to as a clone of aspens. This vast underground root system can live for thousands of years, sprouting new trunks from dormant roots when conditions are just right. This matrix of roots makes aspens hard to eradicate due to the rapid rate of reproduction when the trees finally meet their demise.[5]

This tree analogy is very similar to what occurs with cords. They have evolved and grown over many lifetimes, like the roots of a group of aspens. They may have lain dormant over many years until the conditions were right for the energy to flow again through the cord. Merely cutting the cord will not stop the root from growing back.

The problem with attempting to cut energy cords is they are just like a weed; if we cut off the top, the root is still there. The energy cord will grow back stronger than ever. Cords are also similar in some ways to weeds. A weed is something that grows where we don't want it to grow. We are encouraged to weed our gardens. But here again, there are issues. Many times, when we pull weeds, we fail to remove the root. Then the weeds not only grow back, they spread. How and when we pull weeds influences how long it will take to kill them once and for all. Weeds are easiest to remove when the plants are small and young because they have not yet established their root system, so it is easier to pull the entire root. When weeding, we are encouraged to remove as much of the root system as we can find. But just as in removing cords, it is

---

5.   Hannah Featherman, "Tree Profile: Aspen—So Much More Than a Tree," National Forest Foundation, March 21, 2014, https://www.nationalforests.org/blog/tree-profile-aspen-so -much-more-than-a-tree.

easy to miss tiny pieces, so you may have to repeat the process time and time again.

Cords, like weeds, are opportunistic and will infiltrate open or void spaces. It is important to deny an opportunity for harmful growth. So, what can we do? Fill void spaces with desirable energy. This filling of voids takes away the cord or weed's chance to grow and stops unwanted energy flow because we are filling it with positive energy.

The key is to stop cutting cords. Cord cutting is a harsh concept and an old-fashioned one that has proven unsuccessful. The utilization of obsidian arrowheads to cut cords is prevalent. An obsidian arrowhead is a hand-carved, sharp, black object made of volcanic glass that has cooled and hardened. Many instruct the use of obsidian arrowheads to cut cords. This type of cord cutting is particularly abrasive and unnecessarily invasive. Although it occurs through a visualization process, it is comparable to a knife-happy surgeon. Many surgeons operate because that is the training they received. The surgeon may quickly accept old teachings and never question whether there are alternative methods because that is what they were trained to do.

This unquestioned acceptance occurs with energy workers. Many learn to cut cords, and few question the efficacy because it is taught and repeated so often it is assumed correct. In the process of cord cutting, we often visualize these pieces of volcanic glass cutting the cords. Obsidian is a very harsh and amorphous material. It is recommended to use sparingly with clients who have been through trauma because obsidian will bubble past trauma to the surface where, eventually, it will erupt. While we may choose to entrain with obsidian because it helps to protect and release old trauma during shadow side work, we should always be prepared to deal with the aftermath of working with it.

If we are using obsidian arrowheads for visualization in cord cutting, we are utilizing a sharp volcanic glass that arose from fire and chaos to cut cords of trauma in the auric field. Say what? No. This is a bad idea. First, it will exacerbate the trauma. Second, when that trauma needs dealing with, the practitioner better be skilled in trauma recovery. Third, even if the practitioner follows up the removal with healing, the cord will reattach. The suffering client will have to go through this process all over again. The black obsidian is still ideal for protection, especially paranormal and shadow side work, but not invasive energetic surgery that is not needed when there are other safer methods available.

Lipomas (quite graphically) help us envision why cord cutting is ineffective. A lipoma is a fatty tumor that is almost always benign. Most doctors don't know the cause of lipomas but agree the most likely cause is trauma, perhaps combined with a genetic predisposition to develop lipomas. Typically, lipomas do not require removal unless they grow to such an extent that they are unsightly or uncomfortable. I am acutely aware of the thoughts that go into deciding to remove lipomas. I recently had some removed from my leg. They most certainly were caused by trauma from migraine injections. My doctor and I kept an eye on them for over twenty years. I finally decided to have them removed, knowing the scars would be unsightly and with the warning that they would return.

There are various methods employed to remove lipomas—from needle aspiration to the extreme of surgically cutting them out. If the surgeon removes the entire lipoma, it has a tiny chance of not growing back right away. But guess what? Due to the trauma from the surgery, lipomas almost always begin to grow back in the same spot or right by the incision. Why? Because we are utilizing trauma to heal trauma. This improper use of surgery is illogical. Clearly, when a lipoma grows so large that it is painful or unsightly, surgery might be the answer. However, in almost every instance, the lipoma would still grow back.

Fortunately, lipomas are slow-growing, so the patient isn't aware of the regrowth for quite some time. But the trauma is key. Instead of exploring what trauma occurred to the area and getting to the root cause of why the lipoma developed, the surgeon excises the lipoma and leaves space for more trauma. We immediately see the parallel of cord cutting. There is trauma. So, let's cut it out. Let's not try to heal it when we can cut, cut, cut. But when we read our disclaimers, we will see we are warned about the lipoma returning. Perhaps all cord cutting ceremonies or sessions should come with such a disclaimer.

Again, the problem with cord cutting is evident when we understand oneness. The very idea of disconnecting from The Collective is illogical. Whatever the pain or ailment we feel, we are one with it. We cannot cut ourselves off from it. Even if we convince ourselves we have cut the cord, we will find we have not. Before jumping to the conclusion that I advocate staying in abusive relationships or toxic friendships, consider this. We typically attempt to cut those types of cords once the perpetrator has already harmed us. We have tried to set up boundaries and heal to no avail. Then we resort to cord cutting. Why would this all of a sudden become effective? It would be wonderful if it were, but it is not effective and is often detrimental. However, there is hope. The hope is in healing the dysfunctional cords.

The process of healing through transforming energy is far more effective and far less damaging than cord cutting. No invasive procedure is needed, and The Collective remains whole. No cords are maimed. We opt instead for healing. Healing a cord does not mean we need to reunite with the energy behind the cord. But we will become much more content and frankly less aware of what was bothering us. This process may need repeating until thinking about it no longer affects us. Eventually, true healing will occur. We will dive further into this exercise in chapter 7 as we go deeper into transmutation. Interestingly enough, most people immediately shake their heads in agreement with this proposed change in methods that does away with cutting cords. Most can't and don't deny The Collective, the totality of commonly held beliefs and sentiments that form one consciousness.

Once they think about it, they realize it is time to find a way to heal The Collective as opposed to cutting it apart. It is probably only those of us defensive of the old ways that may dig in our heels (or heals) and insist on staying in the old healing paradigm. Most know it is time to rise up and lean into our energy and begin to transmute it for the highest and best good of all. Cord cutting is not the way to heal The Collective. We are shifting into a higher understanding of the interconnectedness of All That Is. It is barbaric to cut off and sever parts of our whole.

## *Exercise*
## Healing Dysfunctional Cords

This exercise will help you heal dysfunctional cords. It will prove much more effective over time than cord cutting. It takes practice, but it works.

Sit or lie down quietly. Close your eyes and focus on your breath. Bring your attention to whatever issue you want to resolve. Begin to scan your auric field and physical body for the cord of connection. See if you are able to determine where the cord is connected. Proceed with the following steps even if you are unable to determine the location of the cord. Begin to let a picture of the cord form in your mind. Continue to visualize and describe the cord.

If the cord is connected to a situation or person involving pain, the cord will probably look, feel, smell, and even sound disgusting. Begin to sense if energy is flowing through the cord. Is energy flowing in both directions? If not, which way is it flowing? Next, begin to visualize a beautiful color running through the cord. Visualize the cord itself becoming healthy and clean energetically. Then send love through the cord. Love is not finite. It is endless in supply. Sending healthy love through the cord will never deplete your reservoir of love. In fact, it will strengthen it.

Ascertain if the other side of the cord is draining your energy, become aware of it, and send love to stop the energy drainage. If you are so angry or upset that you can't visualize love, go back to sending beautiful light. You may pick any color. Flood the cord with the light of love if you feel negativity is being sent through the cord. Remember, love will prevail even if you don't feel as though it will.

Once completed, bring your hands together in the middle of your chest in a prayerlike position. Give gratitude for the healing of any dysfunctional cords. Ground yourself by feeling the connection from your feet to Mother Earth. You are one with her. Feel energetic roots extending from the bottoms of your feet down into the core of Mother Earth. Wrap the roots around her core and pull some energy back up through your feet and into the rest of your body. Always remember to send some of your gratitude and loving energy through your feet to Mother Earth. Now imagine a place in the cosmos such as a star or a planet. Your higher or soul self may originate from here. Visualize lassoing some of your energy around that star or planet. Give it a little tug. Now you are equally grounded between heaven and earth. When you are ready, bring your attention back into the room and your body. Wiggle your fingers and your toes. When you are ready, slowly and gently open your eyes.

## *Exercise*
## Releasing Old Paradigms

This exercise will help you evolve beyond old ways of seeing and operating in the world. This includes the release of conditioned beliefs that no longer serve you.

Sit or lie down in a quiet place if possible. Close your eyes. Bring your focus to your breath and begin to quiet your mind. Let the thought of the word paradigm drift into your mind's eye. Paradigms are fundamental ways of thinking or believing that are commonly accepted. Conditioned beliefs have much control over our subconscious minds. Begin to think of some of these in your own life. What are some things you have accepted as accurate in your own life? These personal paradigms usually include programs you have had since you were children. Some examples to get you started include: get a spouse because you are pretty but not so smart, always go to church, save your money for a rainy day, I need everyone else's approval, I always need to win.

Now visualize a large box. Step inside the box. This box is your personal paradigm box. Begin to put all of your commonly accepted ways of thinking or believing in this box. This box is a box your subconscious made for you a long time ago. You simply affirmed many things as fact. You might not be able to think of everything during this trip to your personal paradigm box. Realize you can come and visit it anytime. After all, it is always with you. In fact, your old thoughts often feel like they are going to keep you trapped forever. Take one item in your paradigm box right now. Go ahead. Choose one thing. Choose something you have accepted or believed about yourself or the way you interact with the world. This one thing is something you want to change. You want to create a paradigm shift, a different way of looking at it. Take this one thing and carry it outside of your box. Look, there is a ladder right in front of you. Carry the old belief up the ladder. This belief has held you back. Perhaps it was a personal paradigm of thinking that you could never finish school. Someone told you that you were not smart enough.

It is time to shift this particular paradigm. Take whatever it is and see it from a new perspective. You are no longer the child that heard and believed you were too uncoordinated for sports. Whatever it is, take the paradigm and look at it from a different point of view. You can dissect it and study it for as long as you want. But finally, begin to change the form of the paradigm. This step is your personal paradigm shift. Perhaps you were told you would never have a spouse because you were hard to get along with in relationships. No matter what the paradigm, reshape it now. Mold it into whatever form you want it to be for you. Not for anyone else. Just for you. You will not place the paradigm back in the box. The box will eventually have fewer and fewer outmoded beliefs in it. You will no longer be boxed in by these subconscious thoughts that have held you back for far too long. You are stepping into a fresh perspective. This is your own personal paradigm shift.

Once completed, bring your hands together in the middle of your chest in a prayerlike position. Give gratitude for the release of old paradigms or conditioned beliefs that no longer serve you. Ground yourself by feeling the connection from your feet to Mother Earth. You are one with her. Feel energetic roots extending from the bottoms of your feet down into the core of Mother Earth. Wrap the roots around her core and pull some energy back up through your feet and into the rest of your body. Always remember to send some of your gratitude and loving energy through your feet to Mother Earth. Now imagine a place in the cosmos such as a star or a planet. Your higher or soul self may originate from here. Visualize lassoing some of your energy around that star or planet. Give it a little tug. Now you are equally grounded between heaven and earth. When you are ready, bring your attention back into the room and your body. Wiggle your fingers and your toes. When you are ready, slowly and gently open your eyes.

*Chapter Seven*

# Transmute That Shit
## *The Human Black Tourmaline*

The best way to deal with negative energy is to greet it head-on and transmute it. Remember, energy never goes away and cannot be destroyed; it just changes form. Transmutation is the process of changing something into another nature, substance, form, or condition. Many of us speak of or have heard of alchemy. Alchemy is the magical process and science of transmutation. It is changing or combining a substance into something new, often of greater value. Alchemy is not just about changing a physical object such as metal into a different object such as gold. The ultimate alchemy is thoroughly transforming and transmuting ourselves. Therein lies the real secret and magic of transmutation and alchemy. The real magic of transmutation is when we change the form of emotions or anything else that does not serve our highest and best good. The idea of transmuting energy is not new.

There are many varying yet similar teachings regarding transmutation. In Taoism, observers believe that all things are part of the same energy. When we are in flow with that energy, we are at peace. Transmutation, in Taoism, is about realigning with the flow of the Universe or Tao. Buddhism observers achieve transmutation through meditation on mundane knowledge of reality to enlightenment. Enlightenment is also a form of transmutation. In Jainism, transmutation holds that a person must make themselves energetically, spiritually, and finally as physically as light as possible. The reason for this is that when they pass, they pass into pure energy and are at one with the Universe. Most seem to agree that transmutation is raising our beingness to a state of unity with Source. In general, we need to reframe our entire way of thinking and stop always seeking a life free of what we claim is uncomfortable. We need to learn to greet all energy and transmute it when necessary. Some might argue this is just a matter of semantics, but it is so much more. Plus, remember words are also energy, so the words we choose are important.

Many, if not most of us, have heard we are powerfully capable of transforming energy, yet, ironically, cord cutting is still encouraged to disconnect from negative people or energy. This method does not serve us and may even harm us. Crystals are powerful energy beings that we will work with as our sidekicks as we mature into transmuting energy as superheroes rather than cord cutting. We will meet and define these specific sidekicks more in chapters 12 and 13, but for now, a few simple concepts will help us understand why crystals are potent allies. We humans have entropy, better known as chaos. We do not have fixed rates at which we vibrate, and we also do not have fixed internal structures. We entrain to the energy of others, as we have seen. Crystals, however, have fixed oscillation or vibration rates and fixed internal structures. So, they are much less chaotic than us. We entrain easily to crystals. That is the reason we work so efficiently with them.

Take for instance using a black tourmaline. Metaphysical stores and energy workers across the world know that black tourmaline is capable of the mighty feats of absorbing, deflecting, and transmuting negative energy. We use black tourmaline at our front doors, under our car mats, on our office desks, and as jewelry worn every day. Why? Because we are told and may believe that black tourmaline protects us and wards off negative people and energy. Indeed, black tourmaline is useful for dealing with unwanted energy. Remember, we will absorb some energy even when we don't realize it. We may want to deflect such energy so that we don't absorb as much of it. Ultimately, we need to transmute the energy. We have not stepped into the fullness of our abilities as superheroes if we don't realize we can transmute energy. The irony is that we trust black tourmaline to do it, but we don't trust ourselves.

We are also often told to send anything that doesn't serve our best and highest good *to the light*. Sounds good, doesn't it? Well, let's break that down. What are we doing exactly? We need to understand that we are connected to Source. That means *we are the light*. When we send anything to the light, we are part of that light. Since we are part of the light, we are sending the very thing we are trying to get rid of directly to us—the light. We are capable of transmuting that energy ourselves.

Instead of always sending things that don't serve us to the light or sending it to Mother Earth, let us learn to be human black tourmalines and transmute it to light. This new thought may sound like a bizarre proposition because we have been taught many defense mechanisms such as protective bubbles, shields, walls, and yes, cutting cords as discussed in the previous chapters. But these methods, while temporarily effective, are simply Band-Aids. The time has come to embrace our power. We are invited to understand the fundamental, universal laws that everything is energy and everything is connected. Once we grasp these concepts, we slowly put them into practice to become human black tourmalines.

Unequipped Empaths can absorb any type of energy, including that which we have decided does not serve us. Before superhero training, we may not realize just how easy it is to absorb energy the minute we forget to protect ourselves adequately. The absorbing comes so easily to an empath. However, like the black tourmaline, the Empath in Training can deflect negativity with bubbles, shields, suits of armor, or hedges of protection. However, we ultimately have not fully stepped into our power as energetic light beings who are part of Source. We realize how easy it is to absorb the energy, but we stop there. We, desperately at times, begin to search for ways to get rid of the energy we have absorbed. We do not realize our power to transmute the energy until we are Equipped Empaths. When something we perceive as negative comes our way, we need to understand that we cannot only absorb the negative energy but transmute it to positive energy. Then we are an Equipped Empath superhero.

Make no mistake, transmutation will take practice. We are programmed to assign labels to energy: good, bad, positive, negative, and everything in between. While energy does carry a certain vibration that may not align with ours, we choose to assign a label to it. Think of the many times we have felt someone walk into our auric field that immediately makes us feel uncomfortable. We assign judgment to the energy. It is a survival response ingrained deep within every human. Sometimes, however, the label we assign misses the mark. Maybe we think a person is snobbish only to find out they are exhausted. Or perhaps we believe someone doesn't like us, only to find out they have a headache when we meet them. We are perceiving and labeling the energy through our own filters of experience. Most importantly, we must learn to take responsibility for what energy is ours and what we choose to allow to permeate us.

When choosing juries, potential jurors are brought into the courtroom and told to sit in chairs or benches in rows for a process called voir dire. Voir dire is the process of picking the jury. During this process, the likelihood of getting picked to serve on the jury involves several factors, two of which include where the juror is in the order of seating and how much they are willing to talk. If the potential jurors are on the first couple of rows, they are more likely to get picked to serve. I will often tell those on the front two to three rows to imagine putting on their rain ponchos (think Sea World or Blue Man Group) because they are in the splash zone. I explain that this area is the splash zone because they are most likely to get chosen to serve on the jury. I explain that the focus will be more on them than on those in the back rows. More questions and more energy will inevitably come their way. The splash zone scenario is similar to what I tell friends when I call them to vent. I will jokingly warn them to put on their ponchos because I am about to vomit all over them energetically. It is up to them to either not talk to me or put on their poncho. They have a choice. We often just give away our power and our voice. We blame everyone else and how they affect our energy; we are surrendering our authority over what energy we choose to allow into our personal space.

The practice of transmutation begins when we decide to take charge of our own energy and stop blaming everyone else. We can start practicing with small things such as a feeling of irritation. Imagine a coworker is irritating us. We aren't angry; we are just getting irritated. This irritation is our energy; we are not necessarily picking up on their bad mojo. They are just getting on our nerves. As we realize this, there is excellent power in minding our energy that is about to take place. We first pull our energy in tight next to our bodies. *We get a grip.* Then we slowly allow that feeling to permeate us. We absorb it. Now comes the real victory: we change the irritation to a calm sense of intrigue.

We look at the thought-form from outside our body and become mindful of it. We might even grin as we realize we minded the energy. We reframed it. We renamed it. We changed the label. We transmuted it! Our action empowers us and ultimately turns the *dark* to *light*. We call upon our higher selves and Source to help. Remember, *we* are the light. We need to acknowledge and embrace that we are powerfully capable of so much more than we believe or practice. Again, this transmutation of energy takes practice. We are so programmed to protect, clear, or cut bait and run that we have never focused on changing the energy.

We can give Mother Earth some help here. Why do we continually make her do all the work? Yes, she can transmute the energy, but so can we. Consider this as a great way to go green. Recycle energy yourself instead of making Mother Earth do it. If you think about it, we are a little lazy here. Come on, admit it. We talk about helping our Mother, yet we can't be bothered to help transmute energy because it is too tiring for us. This lack of effort is irresponsible of us. We absolutely should recycle every type of energy we can from plastic to negative emotions. They are the same thing, really, right? They are just different forms of energy.

Many energy workers could help with this recycling. In many energy healings or even massage sessions, we will wipe our hands or snap away energy from a client. Then, without realizing it, we either leave it in the room, snapped carelessly to the floor, or we send it to the light or send it to Mother Earth to transmute. Do we see the dilemma? Either way, we will need to transmute it at some point. If we send it to the light, we are sending it to ourselves because we are light and part of Source. If we send it to Mother Earth, eventually she is going to grow weary. Why not help her transmute the energy? Why do we make her do all the work and then turn around and claim we are trying to save her? Always be mindful that the energy never goes away. It changes forms, but it has not gone away. Let's pick that energy up and transform it ourselves.

Customers often come in my stores asking for tools to clear negative energy. SoulTopia, LLC, has tools to help. However, I try to make a point to ask about their own energy. In other words, have they minded their energy, or are they just blaming the energy on everything and everyone else? They will explain how different and unique they are because they are an empath. You see, they don't realize that I hear that from virtually every customer I meet. Now don't get me wrong, I believe most of them are traditional empaths. Empaths are drawn to stores like SoulTopia, LLC. I also think they bring unique giftings to The Collective. My issue comes when they are not embracing their empathy, minding their own energy, or claiming their power. I understand that many are merely Unequipped Empaths. They are either doing the best they can with no training or training that has taught them to use empathy as a crutch. I hope that this book will shed light on the dilemma and encourage all of us to grow into superhero Equipped Empaths.

Just like the Empath Energy Scan in chapter 2 helped us determine what energy belongs to us, now we need something to help us determine where energy from an unknown source is originating. For example, you walk into work and feel some shady shit is going down, but you don't know the source of it. In these instances, you still have the power to absorb and transmute this energy and turn it into vitality for yourself.

As I wrote this book, I told everyone and set the intention to have no drama to deal with during my need for a quiet space. Well, let's just say that the joke was on me. There was one fire after another to put out. I found myself getting anxious, afraid, and angry. However, each time, I realized these were opportunities to put transmutation into practice on a more advanced level. Thank goodness I had practiced on smaller issues. As I sit writing right now, I transmuted significant energy that I encountered earlier in the day. Before I learned to transmute, I would have gone into a depression and gone to bed as my escape. Today this superhero, yes me, transmuted that energy. Consequently, I have more energy and vitality to write.

*Exercise*

## Transmuting Energy When
## You Cannot Detect a Cord of Connection

This exercise will help you transmute energy when you cannot detect a cord of connection. Practice these steps with small irritants in your life so that you are prepared when more substantial obstacles are presented to you. Remember that consistency is the key to successful transmuting.

Make sure you are grounded. Pull your energy in tight against your body. Slowly begin to gather the energy. Imagine pulling all the energy into a ball in front of your heart chakra. This energy includes the good, the bad, and the ugly. If you have already absorbed the energy, as many empaths do, continue following the steps to transmute the energy from within your own body. Visualize the energy and its color, shape, and form. Typically, the color is muted or muddy. Begin to change the former color to a vibrant, beautiful color. Use the first color that comes into your mind. Begin to change the shape and form to something that symbolizes peace, power, or whatever you need from this new energy. Draw the newly transmuted energy into you like oxygen. Imagine placing and absorbing the transmuted energy into any chakra or area you feel needs it.

Feel yourself becoming stronger. Own it. You have transmuted potentially harmful energy into energy you will use for your benefit. When you are ready, open up your wings of transmutation and force field the new energy out to a world in need. You will have plenty to share.

*Exercise*

## Transmuting Energy When
## You Can Identify a Cord of Connection

This exercise will help you transmute energy when you can identify the cord of connection. Practice these steps with small irritants in your life so that you are prepared when more substantial obstacles are presented to you. Remember that consistency is the key to successful transmuting.

Make sure you are grounded. Begin to pull your energy in tight against your body. Start to scan your body and auric field to locate the cord. Where is it attached? Can you envision what it looks like? Begin to change the color you see to a vibrant, beautiful color and send this healing light into and through the cord. Use the first color that comes into your mind.

If you feel any energy coming back to you through the cord, continue to flood the cord with love and the light color you have decided to work with for the healing. Try to flood the cord with loving energy. If you are so angry or hurt that you don't feel you can send any love, flood the cord with a color of your choice. You can even clamp off the cord if you just do not have the power to send anything through the cord. The clamp is a temporary stopgap. As you grow in your routine of this practice, you will feel the need to clamp energy less and less. Begin to change the shape and form to something that symbolizes peace or power or whatever you need from this new energy.

Draw the energy into you like oxygen. As you do, you will feel yourself becoming stronger. Take ownership of this newfound power to manage energy. You have changed the form of energy and now will use it for your benefit.

When you are ready, open up your wings of transmutation and force field the new energy out to a world in need. Never worry about depleting your reservoir of love. You will have plenty to share.

## Example of Utilizing the Steps of Transmutation

You can use this exercise for various situations. The scenario in this exercise will help you practice the steps of transmutation.

You walk into a room, and you realize two people are talking about you. It doesn't matter if you hear them or sense them, you just know. You may have various emotional responses to this. You may feel sad, angry, disappointed, betrayed, jealous, or not affected. But even if you are unaffected, you notice the energy; you feel the shade thrown your way. What can you do to transmute this energy?

Begin to pull back and become the observer. Remember that this is their energy. Perform a scan and tell yourself, "This is not my energy." Realize the protective tools have largely failed you already in this scenario, and the energy has already permeated your auric field. You already absorbed some of their energy the moment you heard or saw them.

If possible, physically walk away from the situation to begin your transmutation process.

Begin to still your mind and connect to your breath. Breath is life and raises our vibration. Take as long as you need until you are ready to deal with the energy they threw at you, the energy you already absorbed.

When you are ready, draw your attention to where you feel an emotion about the situation. Where in your body do you feel it? A punch in the gut? A lump in your throat? A mind of racing thoughts? Continue to draw your attention to that area. Acknowledge the energy you have labeled. I feel angry. I feel sad. I feel jealous. Visualize the color, shape, smell, taste, and texture of the energy.

Next, commence the process of converting the energy. It might be easy to start with the label. Perhaps change it to I am peaceful. I am happy. I am confident. Keep saying the affirmation over and over. Take your thoughts to the area where you feel the energy. Begin to give the energy a beautiful color, shape, smell, taste, and texture.

Repeat the affirmations and mantras you will learn in chapter 9 every time the lower vibration label tries to rear its ugly head.

As you advance in this exercise, you may choose to add tools and side-kicks to aid in your transmutation. Part two of *The Magic of Connection* will introduce you to various tools and sidekicks. You may choose any or all of the tools or sidekicks. You may call on transmutation guides introduced in chapters 10 and 11, hold a transmutation crystal introduced in chapters 12 and 13, work with a transmutation herb introduced in chapter 14, work with a transmutation candle or spell introduced in chapter 15, or work with a transmutation tarot card introduced in chapter 16.

Now, congratulate yourself. You have controlled the absorbed energy and transmuted it. It is not an easy task because we all have failed to practice it for so long. We thought we were empowered, but somewhere deep within us we knew we were stopping short. Begin to feel the vitality of the transformed toxicity. If you are really ready to transmute that shit, place yourself in the presence of the toxicity once more. This may occur through actually being in the presence of the toxicity or by the process of visualization. Slowly sip in the toxic energy and repeat the steps above. This is the ultimate step of taking back your power. This is not stealing energy. This is converting the energy that others meant for ill toward you. Instead of blocking it or hiding from it, now you are transmuting it for your own vitality and use.

Remember, you can still try to protect from these energies using the tools in chapter 4. However, if you forget or they prove ineffective and you absorb energy, then proceed to transmutation. As you advance in the practice of transmutation, you will begin to protect less. You will realize your ability and potential calling to convert pollution into fresh, clean energy. You are recycling dirty energy and converting it to the energy you choose.

Many might claim you will become ill from this practice. On the contrary, you will begin to grow stronger. The transmutation is the critical step to going from victim to superhero. Remember, they were more than willing to give this energy to you. Begin to see it as a gift. *Well, thank you very much for the energy carelessly and maliciously thrown my way. Thank you because I have converted it for my highest and best good.* Now bask in the revitalizing energy.

## Other potential scenarios to practice the process of transmutation

- Someone cuts you off in traffic.
- Someone cuts you off, and they are yelling at you and may even hit your car.
- You hear about a party, and you weren't invited.
- You hear about a party and find out they intentionally left you out.
- You read something on social media you think is directed at you.
- You read something on social media and know it is directed at you.
- Your boss/teacher/partner doesn't acknowledge your hard work.
- Your boss/teacher/partner yells at you despite all of your hard work.
- You are skipped over for a promotion.
- Someone says something hurtful to you or a loved one.
- Someone does something hurtful to you or a loved one.
- The odds seem stacked against you.
- Someone makes a side jab at you.
- Someone spreads rumors about you.
- Someone ignores you.

- Someone picks a fight with you.
- You receive a poorly timed phone call from a telemarketer.
- A cashier is rude to you.
- Your kids come home in a bad mood from school.
- Your kids are disrespectful to you.
- Plans change unexpectedly.
- You have a flat tire and are running late.
- You miss the bus or train on the way to work.
- Security slows you down at the airport.

Keep in mind this is all energy, and you assign the label. You decide how you want to deal with it. Will you mind your energy and grow into the superhero you are meant to be in this life?

The following exercise utilizes crystals to help send healing through cords in order to transmute energy. Black tourmaline and golden sheen obsidian are two crystals of protection that will be used. Black tourmaline will absorb, deflect, and transmute energy. Golden sheen obsidian technically is a type of volcanic glass. It is a gentle form of obsidian due to its golden, warm energy. It will send radiant, golden light through cords to represent and facilitate healing.

## *Exercise*
## Crystal Transmutation

This exercise is a way to learn to begin to transmute energy with crystals.

Sit or lie down in a comfortable position. Close your eyes to begin the steps of transmutation. While doing so, hold a black tourmaline in your dominant hand or releasing hand and hold a golden sheen obsidian in your non-dominant hand or receiving hand. As you recall the experience of absorbing the so-called negative energy, bring your attention to the black tourmaline. The crystal, like you, has absorbed many emotions. You may feel the crystal tingling in your hand due to its piezoelectric property. Sit with this energy for only a few minutes for the first couple of days. After the first couple of days, you can begin to increase your time a few minutes each day.

Eventually, you will get to a point where you no longer focus as much on the negative energy. At that time, this part of the meditation will begin to diminish in time spent.

When sending healing through an energy cord, bring your attention to the golden sheen obsidian. Feel the golden light of healing and transmutation in your hand. As you focus on your crystal, send powerful positive healing and love through the cord of connection. Envision the cord turning into a beautiful golden ribbon. It is shiny and clean and gives you vitality and strength. Eventually, the powerful light of the cord will overwhelm any darkness that tries to come through the cord.

Once completed, bring your hands together in the middle of your chest in a prayerlike position. Give gratitude for the transmutation of any energy that did not serve your highest and best good. Ground yourself by feeling the connection from your feet to Mother Earth. You are one with her. Feel energetic roots extending from the bottoms of your feet down into the core of Mother Earth. Wrap the roots around her core and pull some energy back up through your feet and into the rest of your body. Always remember to send some of your gratitude and loving energy through your feet to Mother Earth. Now imagine a place in the cosmos such as a star or a planet. Your higher or soul self may originate from here. Visualize lassoing some of your energy around that star or planet. Give it a little tug. Now you are equally grounded between heaven and earth. When you are ready, bring your attention back into the room and your body. Wiggle your fingers and your toes. When you are ready, slowly and gently open your eyes.

# Chapter Eight

# Surely Evil People Aren't Included

## *Forgiveness from a Distance*

When we think of staying corded to everyone in The Collective, our minds may immediately go to the extremes. Do we want to absorb the energy of, for instance, a killer? Think of it this way; we probably already have absorbed their energy. No, not probably, we have. Either because we are part of The Collective, so we are ultimately one with the killer, or because we watched a documentary or read a book and absorbed the energy. Maybe we were a victim of a horrible crime. We have absorbed this energy also. In the past, we were instructed to cut cords with the perpetrator. As we saw in chapter 6, cord cutting does not work for the long haul.

What about the killer? The perpetrator? The abuser? The unthinkable one? The monster? Energy transmutation is needed to create charged, new energy in the cord. What can we do when we absorb this horrible energy and feel we cannot live with it anymore? We may try to cut cords. It works for a while, perhaps, yet at some point rears its ugly head, and we have to cut cords again. The surgery of cutting cords weakens us. It doesn't make us stronger. The solution is to take the final step. Transmute the energy. You see, it never is a question of whether we are corded to someone—we are corded. It also is never an issue of absorbing it—we already have absorbed it. It is a question of what we are going to do with it. Remember, energy never goes away; it just changes form. It is up to us how we choose to handle the energy. We can choose to stay in a running, hiding, and cutting mentality, or we can choose to take charge. It becomes a matter of whether we always want to live in defense mode or whether we want to achieve victory.

If we shouldn't cut cords, what should we do instead? What if someone has abused us? What if the wounds go to our very core? What if we are outraged? What if we are scared? Amid great emotion such as fear or anger, it is seemingly impossible to send loving and healing thoughts, but loving and healing thoughts will help our wounds the most. What seems an impossible task will bring remarkable relief and ultimately healing.

If two people are going through a divorce, for example, both may feel a mixture of fear and anger. Perhaps one partner was abusive to the other. The abuse brings up tumultuous emotions every time the abused has to deal with the abuser. Maybe the couple has children, and the abused gets so upset about having to let the children see the abuser that the abused begins to project that fear and angst onto the children. The abused is becoming more and more hurt and the healing is delayed. Eventually, the abused decides it is time to cut cords and may be treated by a well-intentioned healer that attempts to cut cords between the abused and the abuser. But here is the rub. The abused will always have a cord of attachment with the abuser. Not only because of The Collective, but because of the children. Their cords and vines of life remain entwined. Not only in this lifetime but most likely in parallel, past, and future lifetimes. They are entangled. They are corded. No matter how many times the cords are allegedly severed, they will reattach. Are the cords ever permanently cut? No. Just cut down to a nub that grows back over and over again. Many healers address this issue by saying they make sure they extricate all of the cord so it doesn't grow back. They may even say they have filled the area with the soothing balm of love. This explanation is just a realization somewhere in their higher self that is telling the healer there is still an attachment. On some level, we know this explanation is illogical if we believe in the oneness of all.

However, some will believe the cord cutting has legitimately taken place. If it is working for their healing and they need to believe it, then there is no need to convince them otherwise. One way to ascertain whether or not someone has genuinely benefitted from cord cutting is to notice if they are still talking about the person or situation. If they are, chances are the cord has not been cut. However, in some instances, it may be that they healed the cord through the very process espoused in this book. They have transmuted the energy. However, it is more likely the energy flowing through the cord has just dimmed or deactivated. If there is never a trigger, the cord may remain dormant and cause no further harm. What then is the abused to do? The answer is love.

A dear friend of mine, Barbara Chevalier, has a son who was the victim of a horrific crime. It was every parent's worst nightmare. She went out for an evening with her husband while her fourteen-year-old son, Bryan, stayed home playing video games. At some point, Bryan heard a knock at the front door. Thinking it was a friend, Bryan opened the door. He was greeted by a teenage self-professed "serial killer wanna-be." The boy shot Bryan in the chest and back. Bryan was placed in a medically induced coma and on a ventilator. The situation appeared hopeless, but three and a half days later, Bryan emerged from his coma.

The shooter was tried as an adult and sentenced to life in prison. Bryan appeared on a national television news show and shocked the interviewer when he stated he was glad the shooting occurred. The experience had changed him forever, yet neither Bryan, nor his mother, let it take their lives as the shooter had desired. They chose to send healing light to the perpetrator while believing he should also pay for his crimes. They became stronger. They transmuted the negativity and evil of this perpetrator into light and love that they continue to share with others. They also continue to share their choice of love over hate through Barbara's book *Keep Searching for Blue Jays: I'm With You Always.*[6] They are human black tourmalines. They are superheroes of love and light. Forgiveness is what has allowed them to move on and have full lives. Are they still corded energetically to the shooter? Yes, we are all corded to the shooter. Yet the cords between Barbara, Bryan, and the

6. Barbara Chevalier, *Keep Searching for Blue Jays: A Miraculous Account of Life beyond Our World: A True Story* (North Charleston, SC: CreateSpace, 2015), n.p.

shooter are not firing on all cylinders. They would be if hatred went through the cords instead of forgiveness. They chose to send love and moved on with their own lives.

A tragic, yet similar story of forgiveness took place in Dallas, Texas. A police officer went home to her apartment. She was tired and disoriented from a long day. Tragically, she went to an apartment exactly one floor above hers. As she entered what she thought to be her apartment, an unarmed man, eating ice cream, approached her. She shot him and admitted she intended to shoot him. The police officer was convicted of murder. As horrific as the facts of the case were, the standout moment in this trial—the moment reporters say they will never forget—was when the victim's brother made an impact statement after the sentencing. The eighteen-year-old brother of the innocent murdered man told the police officer he forgave her. He then asked the judge if he could hug the officer. The judge agreed, and in a most moving moment, the officer and young man embraced and sobbed. This amazing young man chose to send love through their cords. He took all the negativity from the trial and media frenzy, and he transmuted it in an instant.[7]

Forgiving and healing cords in trauma and systemic, ancestral abuse seems particularly untenable. I have volunteered at and stayed involved in a women's domestic abuse shelter for many years. I must emphatically state that I do not advocate staying with an abuser! I advocate seeking the help of a domestic violence shelter and recommend counseling with a specialist trained in the field of domestic violence to those in such a situation. With that made very clear, I ask again, what about the abused and abuser? Are they still connected? Are they still corded from a distance? When someone who is abused is still very angry with the abuser, the abused may try cutting cords to no avail and eventually realize there will always be a cord or thread of attachment running between them. The abused may begin to realize where in her body she feels the attachment because it has a stronghold. She might finally come to realize that she needs to utilize the exercises in this chapter and chapter 7 instead of implementing the procedure of cutting cords. To find a resolution, she can take the energy from the former abuse and soak it up,

---

7.   F. N. R. Tigg, "Amber Guyger Sentenced to 10 Years in Prison," Complex, Complex Networks, October 3, 2019, https://www.complex.com/life/2019/10/amber-guyger -sentenced-to-10-years-in-prison.

turning it into powerful, positive, and vital energy. In doing so, she'll know she is healthy and empowered, that she is a victim no more, that she is the conqueror. The irony is she will utilize the energy of the very one who hurt her most.

## *Exercise*
## Forgiving from a Distance

This exercise is helpful when you may not feel ready to deal with the difficult and often painful process of transmutation of formidable circumstances. These are the first steps in forgiving from a distance and are useful in conjunction with the Steps for Transmutation from chapter 7. As you work through your healing process, you will be ready to call on the assistance of the tools and sidekicks you will meet in part two of this book. Until then, keep your exercise very simple and focused on self-love.

Sit or lie down in a quiet place if possible. Close your eyes. Bring your focus to your breath and begin to quiet your mind. It is very important to become an observer, be the bystander energetically, and take yourself out of the situation. Remind yourself how deeply you are loved. Begin to send emerald green light and love to your heart chakra. Then send pink light and love to your heart chakra. You may begin to sense these colors swirling together. Sit in this loving energy as long as you so desire.

Once completed, bring your hands together in the middle of your chest in a prayerlike position. Give gratitude for any healing that took place. Ground yourself by feeling the connection from your feet to Mother Earth. You are one with her. Feel energetic roots extending from the bottoms of your feet down into the core of Mother Earth. Wrap the roots around her core and pull some energy back up through your feet and into the rest of your body. Always remember to send some of your gratitude and loving energy through your feet to Mother Earth. Now imagine a place in the cosmos such as a star or a planet. Your higher or soul self may originate from here. Visualize lassoing some of your energy around that star or planet. Give it a little tug. Now you are equally grounded between heaven and earth. When you are ready, bring your attention back into the room and your body. Wiggle your fingers and your toes. When you are ready, slowly and gently open your eyes.

*Part Two*

# The Superhero's Tools and Sidekicks

*"I think a hero is an ordinary individual who finds
the strength to persevere and endure in spite of
overwhelming obstacles." — Christopher Reeve* [8]

8.   Christopher Reeve, *Still Me* (United States: Ballantine Books, 1999), 267.

*Chapter Nine*

# Flip the Script

## *Affirmations, Mantras, and Meditations*
## *for Transmuting Energy*

As we begin learning to transmute energy, we discover transmutation is not as easy as we might have imagined. On our Superhero's Journey, we recognize we need tools to help us. We may be Batman, but we still need our Batmobile. These tools often come in the form of affirmations, mantras, and meditations. We can use them separately or in conjunction to flip the script of our way of dealing with energy. They will finally help us start the process of changing the energy to use to our advantage instead of just protecting against it. Then we can begin to change our energetic story.

When using affirmations, mantras, and meditations, intention setting is of paramount importance to transmuting energy. Remember, due to the Law of Relativity, we assign the labels to the energy. Setting clear and concise intentions will help us be clear about how we want to frame the energy. We are creating our own reality. When we mind our own energy by purposefully setting our intentions, other energy becomes less important. By focusing on our energy, we will change the energy around us.

When and if we feel or sense an energy we do not want, we may or may not know the source of this energy. We now know that somehow, we are corded to this energy. If we can ascertain the source of this cord, we can begin transmutation directly through the cord. If we cannot verify the source of the cord, we begin transmutation of the energy we feel or sense. Both of these exercises are located in chapter 7. Either way, we must know that our ultimate goal is to transmute the energy rather than becoming lost in it.

## Transmutation Affirmations

A transmutation affirmation is a simple, positively worded sentence that instills self-empowerment and leads to a change in the form of energy. We can use transmutation affirmations in different ways, such as speaking or writing them. Whichever way we decide to practice them, it is critical to remember affirmations are positive, and we want to use them consistently. Many of us are straight shooters. In other words, we might not want to say something if we don't believe or feel it is true. We may feel sad and devastated about a situation and feel phony saying, "I am at peace." The best thing to do in these situations is to recognize and acknowledge that we can choose our energy. If that doesn't work and we still feel the words are phony, we can visualize and know that the statement is correct for our true self, our higher self. If we still are not convinced, then we can fake it until we make it because we know that our words have power, and we are ultimately in control of the energy. Affirmations are most effective when stated aloud in front of a mirror every day.

## Transmutation Affirmation Suggestions

- I am energy.
- I am in charge of my energy.
- I can change the form of my energy.
- I am at one with myself.
- I am at one with All.

- I am connected to All.
- I have bright, beautiful cords.
- I am in control of how I define energy.
- I acknowledge how I feel.
- I transform how I feel.
- My energy is mine to manage.
- My energy flows lovingly through my cords.
- I am a high vibration being.
- I send loving light energy through my cords.
- I alter the form of any energy I choose.
- I attract energy I can use.
- I create my reality.
- I am grateful for anyone who sends me any energy I can use.
- I have the power to transmute energy.
- I am vital.
- I am strong.
- I am worthy.
- I am safe.
- I am at peace.

## Transmutation Mantras

A mantra is a process of repeating or chanting the affirmation over and over again. When picking our mantra, we want to recommit to our intention. Once we are clear and concise about the energy we want to transmute, we then should pick a mantra that matches our transmutation intention. The mantra we choose will have a specific vibration; therefore, we want to choose carefully. It should be a mantra that means something to us as opposed to a random mantra. There are mantras we can find that are beautiful and powerful, but we need to make sure they match our transmutation intentions. It is powerful when we create our own mantras because we are the one that puts the intention into every chosen word.

Many times when we desire to transmute energy, we are in some form of pain or discomfort in one of our auric fields. We need to go easy on ourselves and realize we all are new to the transmutation paradigm. A good mantra to begin with might be simply, *I transmute energy with ease and grace.* No matter how upset we feel, we can take a deep breath and start repeating this mantra to ourselves or out loud. We often think we have to be in the ideal, serene setting to do this, but we do not. We may be in the middle of a meeting at work, and someone throws us under the proverbial bus. This time of feeling betrayed is an ideal time to begin our mantra silently—*I transmute energy with ease and grace. I transmute energy with ease and grace. I transmute energy with ease and grace.* Over time we can begin to add to our mantra.

A helpful tool for use with mantras is a mala. A mala is a string or necklace of 108 beads plus a guru bead. The guru bead is the center bead and is a placeholder of sorts. The number 108 stems from the belief in Hinduism that 108 is a sacred number. The mala helps us focus on our intention and sound as we repeat or chant the mantra. Hold the mala in your right hand. Drape it loosely between your index and middle fingers. Begin at the guru bead and use your thumb to count each smaller bead. Pull the smaller bead toward you as you recite your mantra. As you progress around the 108 beads on the mala, you will go into a meditative state. Continue stating or chanting your mantra until you arrive back at the guru bead. Note that sometimes the mala is shortened to 54 beads. At SoulTopia, LLC, we use our beaded bracelets for mantras. The purpose is to focus your intention, much like rosary beads, which are said to have descended from malas.

## Transmutation Mantra Suggestions

- I transmute energy with ease and grace.
- I transmute my own energy.
- I transmute my own energy into love.
- I am the master of my own energy.
- I have sidekicks and tools to help me.
- I am a superhero of transmutation.
- I help Mother Earth by recycling and transmuting energy.

- I will transmute at my own pace.
- I have time and space for transmuting.

## Transmutation Meditations

Transmutation meditation is the process of focusing on the breath, stilling the mind, and visualizing a change in the energy. Learning to transmute energy is a process. Some days, we may convert with ease, while other days we may feel inept. We have been victims of energy for quite some time. We have forgotten our superhero transmuter abilities. We have given away our power to the whims of other energy. However, we are beginning to remember our ability to transmute, but of course, it takes practice. Meditation is an ideal way to program ourselves to mind our own energy and transmute when necessary. As with any meditation, it is best to still our mind so that other energy vibrations may enter it. It is also helpful to pick a particular time or times every day to meditate. However, if we cannot do this, we do not want to let rules stop us from the process. Discipline in the practice will help and will come over time. We can breathe our way into it so that we don't stop before we start. Just as they say in yoga—*this is your practice.* This is your transmutation journey. This is your process of learning how to heal cords. Suggestions are helpful, but you can use any method that works best for you. There is no right or wrong. The goal is to learn to transmute energy for The Collective. Through meditation, we can transmute breath, thought-forms, or cords. The Collective needs healing, and we are the best hope.

The following three exercises will help us add meditation into our transmutation journey.

*Exercise*
## Transmutation of Breath Meditation

This exercise will help you learn to change the form of your breath through a type of meditation known as visualization.

Sit or lie down. Get as comfortable as you can. Close your eyes. Draw your attention to your breath. Focus on your breathing. If a thought comes in, acknowledge it. There is no need to control it. Just gently draw your attention back to your breath. Imagine your breath. What does your breath of life look like at this time? Are you holding your breath? If so, draw your shoulders up to your ears while drawing in a deep breath. Then drop your shoulders and exhale. Repeat this as many times as necessary.

Now see your breath, your essence, filling the space around you. What does this look like at this time? What color is this life energy? Once you see the color, visualize it changing to another color. What color is it now? Once you know this color, you can change the color of your breath again and again. At this point, you can begin to envision two colors. When you are ready, swirl the two colors of your breath together. Does it form a new color, or do you see two distinct colors? When you are ready, begin to develop your breath into a shape. Experiment with the shape of your breath. Do you see a message for you in the color or the shape of your breath? Take note of any messages you receive. When you are ready, collect your energy. Draw your breath back into your own auric field. Bring it into your lungs. Feel the life force within you. Acknowledge the transmutation of energy that has taken place.

Once completed, bring your hands together in the middle of your chest in a prayerlike position. Give gratitude for any transmutation of breath. Ground yourself by feeling the connection from your feet to Mother Earth. You are one with her. Feel energetic roots extending from the bottoms of your feet down into the core of Mother Earth. Wrap the roots around her core and pull some energy back up through your feet and into the rest of your body. Always remember to send some of your gratitude and loving energy through your feet to Mother Earth. Now imagine a place in the cosmos such as a star or a planet. Your higher or soul self may originate from here. Visualize lassoing some of your energy around that star or planet. Give it a little tug. Now you are equally grounded between heaven and earth. When you are ready, bring your attention back into the room and your body. Wiggle your fingers and your toes. When you are ready, slowly and gently open your eyes.

## *Exercise*
## Transmutation of Thought-Form Meditation

This exercise will help you learn to transmute thought-forms through a type of meditation known as visualization.

Sit or lie down. Get as comfortable as you can. Close your eyes. Draw your attention to your breath. Focus on your breathing. If a thought comes in, acknowledge it. There is no need to control it. Just gently draw your attention back to your breath. Slowly and gently draw your attention to the thought-form. Begin to examine the thought-form. What does it look like at this time? Carefully consider this being. What color is it? What shape is it? If it could talk, what would it say? Does it have a texture to it? Does it have a smell? Tell this energy you are going to transmute it. You know that energy never goes away; it merely changes form. You are in charge of this energy. You labeled it, and you created it. You can change it.

Begin to change the color of the thought-form to whatever healing color first comes into your mind. Mold it into a shape that is pleasing to you. What affirming words would you have this energy say to you or others? Smooth the thought-form into a texture that is pleasing to you. Turn it into a beautiful aroma. Begin to feel the low density dissipate and the thought-form begin to vibrate higher and higher. Breathe in and consume as much of the high vibration energy as you choose.

Once completed, bring your hands together in the middle of your chest in a prayerlike position. Give gratitude for any transmutation of thought-forms. Ground yourself by feeling the connection from your feet to Mother Earth. You are one with her. Feel energetic roots extending from the bottoms of your feet down into the core of Mother Earth. Wrap the roots around her core and pull some energy back up through your feet and into the rest of your body. Always remember to send some of your gratitude and loving energy through your feet to Mother Earth. Now imagine a place in the cosmos such as a star or a planet. Your higher or soul self may originate from here. Visualize lassoing some of your energy around that star or planet. Give it a little tug. Now you are equally grounded between heaven and earth. When you are ready, bring your attention back into the room and your body. Wiggle your fingers and your toes. When you are ready, slowly and gently open your eyes.

## *Exercise*
## Transmutation of Cords Meditation

This exercise will help you transmute energy in your cords through a type of meditation known as visualization.

Sit or lie down. Get as comfortable as you can. Close your eyes. Draw your attention to your breath. Focus on your breathing. If a thought comes in, acknowledge it. Begin to pull your energy in tight against your body. Scan your body and auric field to locate the cord. Remember that sometimes cords will attach in random spots. Just keep scanning and trust your instincts. Once you have found the cord, what does it look like at this time? Cords that require healing may not look appealing. That is alright. You are about to heal the cord. Begin to change the former color to a vibrant, beautiful color and send this healing light into and through the cord. Use the first color that comes into your mind. If you feel any energy coming back to you through the cord, try to flood the cord with loving energy. If you are so angry or hurt that you don't feel you can send any love, you can flood the cord with a color of your choice. As a last resort, you can even clamp off the cord if you do not have the power at this moment to send anything through the cord. The clamp is a temporary stopgap. As you grow in your routine of this practice, you will feel the need to clamp energy less and less.

Begin to change the shape and form to something that symbolizes peace, power, or whatever you need from this new energy. Draw the energy into you like oxygen. Feel yourself becoming stronger. Own it. You have changed the form of energy and now will use it for your benefit. The energy was offered to you, and now that you have transmuted it, you will use it for your benefit. When you are ready, open up your wings of transmutation and force field the new energy out to a world in need. You will have plenty to share.

Once completed, bring your hands together in the middle of your chest in a prayerlike position. Give gratitude for any transmutation of cords. Ground yourself by feeling the connection from your feet to Mother Earth. You are one with her. Feel energetic roots extending from the bottoms of your feet down into the core of Mother Earth. Wrap the roots around her core and pull some energy back up through your feet and into the rest of your body. Always remember to send some of your gratitude and loving energy through your feet to Mother Earth. Now imagine a place in the cosmos such as a star or a planet. Your higher or soul self may originate from here. Visualize lasso-ing some of your energy around that star or planet. Give it a little tug. Now you are equally grounded between heaven and earth. When you are ready, bring your attention back into the room and your body. Wiggle your fingers and your toes. When you are ready, slowly and gently open your eyes.

*Chapter Ten*

# Show Me the Way
### Guides for Transmuting Energy

O n our Superhero's Journey, we often need sidekicks to help point us to our higher selves, which are connected to everyone else, and, in turn, are connected to Source. They will often help us overcome obstacles and challenges we face along our journey. We need a Robin to our Batman, a Wonder Girl to our Wonder Woman, or a Rick Jones to our Captain America. The sidekicks we will employ are often referred to as gods, goddesses, angels, archangels, spirit guides, ascended masters, or ancestors. The more we explore the idea of tapping into our higher selves, the more we may ask, "Do we need guides?" After all, guides are just that; they guide and help us along our paths. They do not seek worship; instead, they want to show us the way. We certainly may choose to honor and thank them, but worship is not required. How we revere and honor them is a personal choice. While guides might be of service, they are not mandatory once we have transcended into the understanding of our higher selves being one with All That Is, which includes a direct source to Divine, or some deity. These guides are much like bumper pads in bowling. They keep us on track and guide us to Source just like the bumper pads guide the bowling ball to the bowling pins.

We are ready for our call to adventure and subsequent training but may not feel confident about the process of transmutation. We may need to call on sidekicks for assistance. Some may find it hard to stop using terminology such as ascended masters or goddesses. This difficulty may be due to fear of disrespect. We may lose that fear as we grow in our understanding of oneness, but it will take more time for some than for others. For that reason, some labels are included in the descriptions below. The main thing to remember is that we are embracing our ability to become the superheroes of our energy. Yet sometimes we will need assistance. Never fear—our sidekicks are here.

Here are some examples of who we might call on for assistance with transmuting energy. While there are many other sidekicks, these are chosen to help get us started because they are known to specifically help with transmutation. Please note: Archangels are androgynous, but often their energy will feel more masculine or feminine. To the extent a pronoun identifier is used, it is to describe the way the energy feels.

## Hermes, Thoth, and Hermes Trismegistus

Purpose: boundaries, transitions, alchemy, astrology

The Roman god Hermes is one of the twelve Olympian gods. His primary job is delivering messages to the other gods. But along with other purposes, he is the god of boundaries and transitions. He is quick footed and confident in his work. Thoth is one of the most important Egyptian deities as the Egyptian god of writing, magic, wisdom, equilibrium, balance, and the moon. The Greeks identified Hermes with Thoth and named him Hermes Trismegistus, meaning *thrice-greatest*. He knew the three parts of the wisdom of the universe: alchemy, astrology, and theurgy. As a scribe of the gods, Hermes is credited with all Greek sacred books. These books were called hermetic. At some point, alchemy became known as the Hermetic Arts.[9]

We can call upon this deity of alchemy and transmutation by whatever name resonates with us. This sidekick assists us with transmutation because

---

9. David Hill, "Spiritual Alchemy for Beginners," Esoteric Meanings, October 21, 2016, http://www.esotericmeanings.com/spiritual-alchemy/.

he helps us recognize the boundaries of matter and form and also how they can be magically altered. When we want to begin working on transmuting energy and don't know how to get started, Hermes is perfect for showing us the way. In this respect, he is a mentor of sorts, which makes him a great sidekick.

## Isis and Osiris

Purpose: perseverance, overcoming, alchemy, transmutation

The story of Isis and Osiris is an excellent example of the alchemical and transmutation process. Osiris was dismembered and thrown into the sea, but his wife, Isis, found all of his bodily parts, except one, and reassembled him. Isis didn't give up on the missing piece because it was needed to make their future child Horus. Isis made the penis out of gold. Fashioning the penis from gold was the actual alchemical process of dissolving and rejoining.

Isis and Osiris are excellent to call on when we feel we need transmutation in our lives. The situation with Isis and Osiris seemed hopeless. Most would have given up. When we want to give up is the exact time to call upon them. Isis will help us persevere. Osiris will remind us that even if we feel we can never be put back together, we can. We can overcome any obstacle through transmutation.

## Sekhmet

Purpose: protection, healing, safety

Sekhmet is an Egyptian goddess. While she is a goddess of great wrath, she is also a goddess of protection and healing. She has the head of a lion. A lion does not see everything as prey, just things that threaten it. Sometimes we are threatened by something, and we do not know why. We only know there is imminent danger. Our natural instinct of fight or flight kicks in when we are in such a knowing space.

We can call upon Sekhmet as a sidekick when we feel there is an unhealthy cord of connection in the root chakra. We may not even know the full story, but we know we feel threatened. She will help us send healing through the cord when we think we are prey to someone else's malicious intentions. With Sekhmet by our side, we will feel courageous and victorious.

## Merlin the Wizard

Purpose: divination, wizardry, alchemy, shape-shifting

Merlin the Wizard has many magical and mystical powers. He is one of the most powerful and transformative energy forces with whom humans have come into contact. Merlin served as advisor to King Arthur, encouraging him to unite Britain, begin the Round Table, and pursue the Holy Grail. He also placed the violet flame in Camelot and spent an incarnation as Saint Germain, keeper of the violet flame.

He is perfect to call upon as a transmutation sidekick because he is the quintessential alchemist and shape-shifter. However, he doesn't just change clothes or form; Merlin changes his very essence.[10] He is a true transmuter of energy with no need for additional tools. He simply moves energy with his mind. Interestingly, Archangel Raziel is the Merlin of archangels.

## The Morrigan

Purpose: magic, shape-shifting, helps when battling others

The Morrigan is a Celt goddess of war. The Celts had many beliefs surrounding warfare as it was common to them. The Morrigan is a complicated goddess, but for our purposes, it is most important to know that she utilized transmutation in the form of magic and shape-shifting to achieve her objectives. The Morrigan would often shape-shift into a beautiful woman, raven, crow, wolf, eel, cow, or any other being while in battle.

She is the sidekick to turn to when transmutation seems impossible. When we feel we are continually battling ourselves or someone else, we can turn to her for help. She will show us different methods to employ in our transmutation arsenal, helping us realize that once we push through the emotions and stop labeling the energy, we will emerge victorious in battle.

## Saint Germain

Purpose: using the violet flame of transmutation, helping us raise our vibration

Saint Germain lived many lifetimes and was a prophet to many historical figures.[11] Saint Germain can impart to us the violet flame of transmutation.

---

10. Stephen Knight. *Merlin: Knowledge and Power through the Ages*. Ithaca; London: Cornell University Press, 2009. Accessed May 17, 2020. www.jstor.org/stable/10.7591/j .ctv75d4tw.

11. Godfre' Ray King [pseud.], *Unveiled Mysteries* (Chicago, IL: Saint Germain Press, 1934), n.p.

The violet flame changes so-called negative energy into positive energy. It changes the vibration of the energy or how fast energy moves back and forth. It transmutes this energy at the atomic level, where energy is dense. It speeds up the oscillation until we are vibrating at a higher level.

We can use the violet flame to transmute energy to raise our vibration. Saint Germain helps us when we want to transmute energy that we deem negative. Remember that cording occurs between all types of energies, including a person to a situation. Saint Germain helps when we are corded to situational energy, such as memories or occurrences involving specific places.

## Archangel Zadkiel

Purpose: compassion, transmutation through forgiveness, calming influence

Zadkiel is the archangel of compassion and forgiveness. His name means *righteousness of God*. He helps us transmute through forgiveness. He has a dark blue aura and calming energy.

We can call upon Zadkiel as a sidekick whenever we desire to change something through transmutation. His calming influence is particularly helpful when we are too upset to believe we want to forgive either ourselves or anyone else. He will help us find the compassion we need to forgive. Once we have Zadkiel by our side, we will find it easier to send healing through the cords.

## Archangel Raziel

Purpose: sacred geometry, quantum physics, esoteric secrets, clears karmic residue, heals cords, manifestation, magic

Raziel is the archangel of spiritual insight. His name means *secret of God*. Archangel Raziel has an extremely high intellectual vibration. His energy is exceptionally subtle, so we must listen carefully with our entire being to connect to him. Many maintain that Metatron is the archangel who governs sacred geometry due to Metatron's cube. In actuality, Raziel connects us to sacred geometry, quantum physics, and esoteric secrets. Raziel is known as the Merlin of Archangels. His affiliation with Merlin is why he is the angel of manifestation and magic. Raziel's aura is that of a rainbow of known and unknown colors.

We can call upon Archangel Raziel when we want to clear karmic residue in our cords. Karmic residue is any karma that is lingering in our lives. Raziel will also help us understand things about situations that have remained mysterious to us in the past. Perhaps we could not understand why someone treated us with disrespect. He will illuminate the karma behind the relationship so that the cord may heal.

## Archangel Azrael

Purpose: comforts those transitioning, leads those transitioning to the light, comforts the grieving

Azrael is the archangel of death, comfort, and grief. Azrael means *whom God comforts*. He often gets a bad rap as the angel of death with a black hood and sickle. This unfortunate reputation is merely due to the fear of the unknown. He is actually an archangel of compassion and comfort to anyone facing death. Azrael comforts those transitioning and those left to grieve. This compassionate angel gently directs us to the light. Azrael also helps those who are in the business of death and dying, such as doctors, nurses, chaplains, funeral home directors, ministers, and hospice caregivers. However, Archangel Azrael can also assist with any type of grief. Loss of any kind often leads to grief.

We remain corded to everything we lose in life. The strength of the cording may even grow stronger during the mourning process. Part of our transmutation of those cords of connection is to send healing and, eventually, this cord will recede and become dormant. It will, however, take time. In the meantime, having a sidekick to help us is invaluable. Archangel Azrael will help us send a soft, gentle yellow light through the cord. This help from him brings soothing comfort to both sides of the cord. It is very comforting to know we can call on such a helper in times of great sadness, grief, and despair.

## Solomon

Purpose: master magician, alchemist, divine symbols, sigils, talismans for transmutation, musician, poet, architect, transmutation through creative expression

King Solomon is a master magician and alchemist. His divinely inspired symbols, sigils, and talismans help transmute all types of energy, including harmful into protective or mundane into divine. He was a musician, poet, and even an architect. Much like the Egyptian pyramids, when constructing the Holy Temple, otherwise known as Solomon's Temple, Solomon was mindful of the materials and designs he used. The materials and construction brought about direct transmutation. Furthermore, anything he ever made is just as powerful now as when he created it.

We can call upon King Solomon when we need help expressing and transmuting our experiences through art, music, and poetry, as he represents transmutation through creative expression. As the magical architect, Solomon will also help us build or rebuild relationships with those we choose. Because everything Solomon ever touched or built still retains its magic, Solomon truly had the magic touch. He is the perfect sidekick to help us mindfully work on our connections with others and the tangible representations of those connections.

## Blue Tara

Purpose: transmutes anger, ferocious, intolerant of nonsense, obstacle destroyer, brings motivation

Blue Tara is one of twenty-one Taras in the Buddhist tradition. A Tara is a female bodhisattva, or one seeking enlightenment. She is also commonly referred to as the mother of liberation.

We can call upon Blue Tara for the transmutation of anger when we are feeling overwhelmingly irate. She will help remove any fear we have of potential enemies and remove all obstacles on our path to enlightenment and spiritual awakening. But we need to know that Blue Tara can be ferocious and does not abide nonsense. When working with her, we must not make any excuses. Blue Tara gets to the point and helps us feel the anger and then turns that anger into energy we can use, such as vitality or drive.

## Oya

Purpose: change, release, empowerment, storms, chaos to facilitate transmutation

The Yoruba out of Nigeria introduced us to this fierce orisha of transmutation. Oya is all about change, release, and empowerment. This orisha of storm and change comes blowing into our lives to help us know that we all possess the power to change even when we are resistant to it.

If we call on Oya, we need to be warned. She does not mess around. She will not let us sit and do nothing. She will create a storm inside us to spur a desire for change. If we remain resistant to necessary change, make no mistake, Oya will bring the chaos required to knock us to our knees so that we might rise victorious. Call upon Oya when there is healing needed in our cords of connection, which we have resisted but finally admit need repair. On the other hand, when there is destructive or abusive energy directed toward us, she will waste no time in kicking ass. She will also help us collect that energy and change it into something that serves us, bringing us to a place where we are empowered, energetic transmuters of energy.

## Kali

Purpose: death, destruction, time, change, transformation, creation

This fierce Hindu goddess is another excellent sidekick to help us transmute energy. She is often put in the evil goddess category because she definitely can and will wield death and destruction. It is interesting to note that assassins in India worshiped her. They were known as *thuggees*, which is the origin of the term *thug*. This worship is somewhat the same as the worship of Santa Muerte. Santa Muerte, like death, does not ever discriminate. She knows that death comes to us all and she judges no one. In India, all goddesses fold into one called Devi. Kali is one of the forms of Devi that is the most beloved in India. She is the goddess of time, change, and transformation.

Like Santa Muerte, those who work with Kali realize that death brings transmutation in a different form. Kali only destroys what needs destroying. Once destroyed, a new creation can begin. This insight into Kali helps us see her differently. She is the goddess of creation as much as she is the goddess of destruction. She destroys anything that no longer serves us. Of course, this may bring about fear. Fear is a mighty destroyer in and of itself.

We can call on Kali to give us the courage to defeat these fear illusions, including the fear of transmutation. Like Oya, call on Kali to transmute the energy of abusive relationships and provide the courage to manifest a new life. Through Kali, we can learn to meet energy we label as negative head-on. Then we can absorb that energy and transmute it for our empowerment. We are now taking control of the energy and releasing it by changing the form of it. We are truly operating as a superhero, and our sidekick is Kali.

## Cerridwen

Purpose: shape-shifting, wise, keeper of the cauldron, change, transformational healing

Cerridwen is a Welsh, shape-shifting triple goddess. Although a triple goddess embodies all stages of womanhood, the Maiden (virgin), the Mother, and the Crone (wise), Cerridwen manifests primarily in the crone stage. Hence, she is considered to carry the wisdom and experience of her years. She is also the keeper of the cauldron. The cauldron represents the womb and the place where all life, knowledge, and magical inspiration takes place.

Cerridwen is helpful to us when change is needed but we are resistant to it. We can embrace change as the catalyst to move us forward in our lives, or we can resist it and make the transmutation process more difficult. Fortunately, we have Cerridwen to help us move along with wisdom and discernment. When change comes into our lives, we may need to work on some of the ties that hold us back. Sending transformational healing to the ties that bind us will help us move forward. If we remember to call upon Cerridwen when we are scared of change, we will have a great sidekick to transmute ourselves into our next stage of life without always looking back at the past. We will be able to live in the moment, knowing that it will become the past.

## Hecate

Purpose: witchcraft, magic, crossroads, decision making, clarity, discernment

Hecate is a Greek goddess of witchcraft, magic, doorways, crossroads, and the moon. She is associated with nighttime and carries a torch. She is also known to have her own hellhounds. Creatures of the night, such as ravens, owls, and crows are sacred to her. She deals with what we may think of as the darker side of life, but she is capable of both good and evil. Black and silver are colors associated with Hecate.

When we are at a critical point of decision making, it behooves us to call upon Hecate's help. Life is full of crossroads. We may feel at a crossroads as to whether a person should remain in our lives or not. We may feel we are receiving conflicting information, or we cannot get to the bottom of the facts surrounding an issue. This confusion can cause us tremendous stress with the situation or person to which the circumstances are corded. It is at this very time that we most need clarity. Hecate will help bring us clarity and discernment. We may even solicit her help in standing with us at the crossroad of our decision. This help will give us time to decide how and when to transmute the energy. Hecate's energy can be summoned if we visualize black and silver energy running through cords.

## Tesla

Purpose: understands feeling underappreciated, helps recharge our spark, claim our genius

Many times, we are misled into thinking only ancient lore will lead us to our sidekicks. This way of thinking is another common misconception that *The Magic of Connection* encourages us to dismiss. We can call upon any sidekick that guides or helps us in whatever way we need assistance. For help with transmutation, Tesla is one such helper. Nikola Tesla was a Yugoslavian immigrant to the United States via Ellis Island. Tesla eventually worked for Thomas Edison. After leaving The Edison Company, the two ultimately diverged in opinions on many things, including electricity. Edison advocated direct current while Tesla insisted on alternating current. Although Tesla was recognized for his genius, he endured many hardships regarding his patents and finances. He died a hermit and penniless. However, alternating current is the reason we can afford much of the electricity we use today.

Tesla is the sidekick we can call upon when we feel we are underappreciated or go unnoticed. We may have great inspiration and ideas only to have them overshadowed or dismissed. Tesla will help guide us through this time and help us recharge our own spark. We can also send this spark through cords of connection when we feel we need a chance to express our own genius.

## *Exercise*
### Selecting and Utilizing Sidekicks

This exercise will help you select and utilize sidekicks on your Superhero's Journey.

Think of an area in your life where you may need help with a cord of connection. Write down the first one that comes to mind. Now think of a sidekick to help you; the ones listed in this chapter are ideal for cord work and transmutation.

Once you select a sidekick, begin to develop a relationship with them like you would a new friend. Ask questions of them, and be sure to listen and watch for signs of their presence in your life. Allow them to intervene in situations where you need help changing or transforming energy in the area of concern. Think of the energy of this sidekick going before you when you have to deal with matters surrounding the issue. Most importantly, use the techniques learned in chapters 6 and 7 to heal any cords that need repair.

If one of the listed sidekicks does not seem to fit your situation, you can think of one of your own. Just as Tesla may seem an unlikely sidekick, think of anyone that might be the perfect guide for you in this situation. All too often, we leave the business of picking sidekicks to someone else. We ask a healer or intuitive to tell us who guides us. While that might be helpful, you can discover your own sidekick for each unique situation that involves working with transmuting cords.

Remember, you are also corded to your sidekicks. You will merely turn up the connection. It is acceptable to choose your sidekicks rather than just waiting for them to appear to you or choose you. Assuming the sidekick is not one previously listed in this chapter, you might want to learn a little about their history as well as the qualities they possess to grasp how to best work with them.

*Chapter Eleven*

# Animal Instinct
## *Animal Guides for Transmutation*

A nimal guides may work with us for a lifetime or help us for a designated time regarding specific situations. The following animal guides are suggested sidekicks to help us on our Superhero's Journey. They may also give us signs letting us know when and what type of healing needs to take place in our cords. Here are some examples of who we might call on for assistance with transmuting energy. While there are many other sidekicks, these are chosen to help get us started because they are known to specifically help with transmutation. We can also discover our own animal sidekicks to help us.

### Bat
Purpose: highly sensitive, strong family ties, shape-shifters, communication, socialization

The only mammal in the world that can fly, Bat is flexible and swift. Bats live in roosts with protected nooks and crannies such as caves. Since good roosts are hard to come by, they are often shared by millions of bats, all roosting upside down. Because they roost upside down, bats see things from a different perspective. They utilize high pitched echolocation for determining location and communicating with one another. Bats are also associated with change, rebirth, shape-shifting, and transmutation.

Bat is an ideal sidekick to call upon when dealing with cord issues associated with family members. Bat will help us with communication so we can heal cords of connection. Bat is also useful when we need to look at a connection with a different perspective.

## Crow/Raven

Purpose: mysteries, magic, transformation, alchemy, shape-shifting

Crows and ravens are very similar. Ravens are larger and tend to travel in pairs while crows are smaller and tend to travel in larger groups. Some see these birds as bad omens; however, they are actually a sign of magic.

This is why they are useful as transmutation sidekicks. Both Crow and Raven will help us learn to believe in our ability to transmute energy. They will help us realize we can all perform alchemy. We can change the form of energy without initiation into any secret societies. We are all part of *The Magic of Connection*. Call upon Crow and Raven as sidekicks to help send magic through the cords. You don't have to understand it, just trust that the magic will work.

## Snake

Purpose: life out of death, transmutation, alchemy, complete consumption of prey, shedding of skin

Snake energy has long been viewed as a symbol of transmutation. Ouroboros is a snake in the shape of a lemniscate, or infinity symbol, eating its own tail. Snake represents life out of death and is a universal symbol of transmutation and alchemy. All snakes can swallow their prey whole. The teeth of a snake are not used for chewing but for grabbing and holding. This ability to completely consume the being is closely tied to transmutation. We can use Snake energy to help us know that we can consume transmuted energy in its entirety. Snake then shows us how to grow as our skin becomes thicker. While all animals and even humans shed skin, it is more noticeable in a snake because snakes only shed their skin periodically and often in one piece. This shedding or molting is representative of the release we experience after transmutation. Snakeskin does not stretch as snakes grow. Instead, the old skin is shed to allow for growth. Further, the shedding serves to rid the snake of parasites that may have attached to it.

As transmuters of energy, it is important for us to work with Snake energy. In the process of absorbing and transmuting energy, we will experience growth. Snake will help us shed our old ways or anything we have failed to transmute. This way, we can grow into a connection with our higher self.

## Scorpion

Purpose: passionate, survivors, courageous, resilient, reinventors

Scorpions are determined and passionate survivors. They existed since before the time of dinosaurs. Researchers have frozen scorpions overnight and put them in the sun the next day to see what would occur. They were stunned when the scorpions thawed out and walked away. They are most certainly tenacious. Scorpions are so damned determined to persevere that they can live on one insect a year.[12]

Scorpion is the perfect sidekick to help us with transmutation when we feel like we have been through hell. Scorpion gives us unshakeable courage and resilience to stand up to the energy flowing through the cord. Even if the energy flowing through the cord toward us is strong and detrimental, Scorpion will give us mighty resolve to transmute the energy and send powerful golden light that will overcome any forces flowing through the cord toward us. Scorpion will also help us reinvent ourselves into more tenacious superheroes, if needed, after healing the cord.

## Inchworm and Silkworm

Purpose: small steps, measured movements, small but resilient

Inchworms begin as eggs laid on branches of trees. Once hatched, the larvae are inchworms. They move by inching forward. Eventually, using silk threads, the larvae lower themselves to the ground and burrow under dirt or leaves. They spin a cocoon until they are ready to emerge as adult moths.

---

12. "Scorpions," National Geographic, September 24, 2018, https://www.national geographic.com/animals/invertebrates/group/scorpions/.

Silkworms are also the larvae of moths. There are two types: one eats mulberry leaves, and one eats oak leaves. All butterfly and moth caterpillars produce silk, as do spiders and some other insects. But only silkworms make the beautiful, luxurious fiber that is made into commercial silk. They also go through the transmutation process of becoming adult moths.

We can call upon Inchworm or Silkworm as a sidekick when we need to take small steps; when we are hesitant or unsure about change and want to take our time. Small, measured movement is the type of methodical action that helps us ease into transition. Real transmutation often does not take place in an instant. It happens after we sit with our feelings. The anger, fear, and disappointment are real. We must acknowledge these feelings. Then we become an observer of the pain instead of a participant. Once we can pull ourselves out of the story, we are ready to begin our metamorphosis. Our sidekick Inchworm or Silkworm reminds us that although we may seem small, we are resilient.

## Butterfly

Purpose: transformation, transmutation, complete altering of energy, heal ancestral cords

There are many kinds of butterflies, but they all have one thing in common: they go through stages of transformation. Butterflies go through four stages of transformation: egg, larvae (caterpillar), pupa (chrysalis), and adult. These stages of transformation ultimately lead to the transmutation from an egg to a butterfly. Another exciting way butterflies represent transmutation is their ability to evolve their color. In a study at Yale University, scientists discovered that certain butterflies were changing colors. The study explained that the color could be changed by a difficult process of altering pigment or by the easier way of adjusting wing structure or other body parts that reflect light. Butterflies were transmuting their color the easier way. They were changing their wings, and thereby colors, in some cases in as few as six generations.[13] This color change illustrates how we can easily evolve into change if we so choose.

---

13.   Elizabeth Preston, "It Only Takes Six Generations to Turn a Brown Butterfly Purple," Discover, August 8, 2014, https://www.discovermagazine.com/planet-earth/it-only -takes-six-generations-to-turn-a-brown-butterfly-purple.

It is important to note that we are doing more than transforming the energy when we transmute energy. Although transformation may be part of transmutation, the two are different. When we transform energy, the energy is still the same. It merely takes a different form and is dressed differently. We may act differently, we may even feel differently, but the energy is still the same. However, we want to stop dressing up the energy, and we want to change it completely. Otherwise, we will become exhausted by keeping up with the costume changes. For example, if we are in a job where we are working with an annoying team, we will accentuate the positive and put on our happy face to get through the situation.

Meanwhile, our internal feelings regarding the situation stay the same, and we are miserable. Real transmutation is a complete and total altering of the energy. This involves changing the energy and beginning to truly enjoy the job instead of continuing to put on a phony, happy face with your team. It is not quitting or running. It is making the energy work for you. There is no going back to what was. The caterpillar does not return to its chrysalis. It transmutes into a completely new being. It is a being that is beautiful and free.

Butterfly is the sidekick to call upon when we recognize a cord healing may require a long process. Butterfly will help us transmute any and every type of energy for the long haul. It will help us through each stage of the transmutation process.

Butterfly is also helpful for ancestral cycles that need healing. Traditionally, ancestral healing has been handled through cord cutting; however, we know this type of energy work does not last. Butterfly reminds us we are all connected, and they are ideal sidekicks to heal ancestral cycles in cords of connection.

## Komodo Dragon

Purpose: brave, patient, overcomer of any obstacle

Komodo dragons are the world's heaviest lizards, weighing in at about three hundred pounds. They are carnivores and will eat just about anything. The Komodo dragon is brave enough to take anything on or tackle any situation. They have the patience to wait for their venom to take effect on their prey.[14] The venom is highly toxic, and the bite of a Komodo dragon is not pleasant, either, as it is more like a tear that leaves a gaping hole, allowing the venom to seep into the wound. Komodo dragons mate as male and female, but females can also reproduce asexually. However, the resulting offspring of such reproduction is only male Komodo dragons, which threatens the survival of the species.

Work with Komodo Dragon as a sidekick when bravery is needed. They will help us realize we can overcome any obstacle presented by a cord of connection. Komodo Dragon also reminds us that sometimes great patience is necessary to transmute energy. Dragon energy is considered some of the most potent animal totem energy to work with in any situation. Primarily, it is important to note that how Komodo dragons choose to mate leads to very different outcomes. Call on Komodo Dragon when deciding which type of cord work is needed.

## Phoenix

Purpose: epitome of transmutation, conquer fear, rise as a better person, unique

The phoenix originates from ancient lore. They are huge, like eagles, and well known to be associated with the worship of the Egyptian god of the sun, Ra. Only one phoenix existed at a time and usually lived for at least five hundred years. As its death approached, the phoenix would build a nest, set it on fire, and become consumed by the flame. Phoenix would emerge reborn from the ashes and flame.[15]

Phoenix is the epitome of transmutation. Phoenix will help us conquer our fears and emotions to become a better version of ourselves. We will know that the transformation, while it may feel like an ending, is actually a transmutation into a new beginning. Phoenix can be used for self-imposed healing or externally imposed situations that require change. It reminds us that although we are all one, no one is exactly like us. We have emerged reborn, and that is our superpower.

14.   "Komodo Dragon," National Geographic, accessed March 20, 2020, https://www.nationalgeographic.com/animals/reptiles/k/komodo-dragon/.

15.   "Phoenix: Mythological Bird," Encyclopaedia Britannica, accessed May 17, 2020, https://www.britannica.com/topic/phoenix-mythological-bird.

## *Exercise*
## Selecting Animal Sidekicks

This exercise will help you choose animal sidekicks to work with in general or specific situations.

Think of an area in your life where you may need help with a cord of connection. Write down the first one that comes to mind. Now think of a sidekick to help you; the ones listed in this chapter are ideal for cord work and transmutation.

Once you select a sidekick, begin to develop a relationship with them like you would a new friend. Ask them questions and be sure to listen and watch for signs of their presence in your life. Allow them to intervene in situations where you need help changing or transforming energy in the area of concern. Think of the energy of this sidekick going before you when you have to deal with matters surrounding the issue. Most importantly, use the techniques learned in chapters 6 and 7 to heal any cords that need repair.

If one of the listed sidekicks does not seem to fit your situation, you can think of one of your own. All too often, we leave the business of picking sidekicks to someone else. We ask a healer or intuitive to tell us who guides us. While that might be helpful, you can discover your own sidekick for each unique situation involving working with transmuting cords.

Remember, you are also corded to your sidekicks. You will merely turn up the connection. It is acceptable to choose your sidekicks rather than just waiting for them to appear to you or choose you. Assuming the sidekick is not one previously listed in this chapter, you might want to learn a little about their history as well as the qualities they possess to fully grasp how to best work with them.

## *Exercise*
## Animal Guide Transmutation

This exercise will help you experience the energy of all of the animal transmutation sidekicks.

Sit or lie down in a comfortable position. Close your eyes. Begin to bring your focus to your breath. As your breathing begins to slow down, transport yourself to a safe space. This safe space is your special place of meditation.

Draw your attention to the cord of connection that you wish to transmute. As you look around your sacred space with your mind's eye, you notice Bat hanging in the corner. Do not become alarmed. Bat is merely roosting in its safe space. It is thinking of things from a different perspective and has shown up to help you do the same. Then Raven lands on your shoulder. You are not startled. Raven feels familiar and reminds you that you can work magic. Next, you notice Snake on the ground. Snake has shown up to help you shed anything that no longer serves you. Snake will also help you grow a thicker skin as you go through transmuting energy. This thicker skin serves as temporary protection so that you don't have to harden your heart.

Next, you see Scorpion. Scorpion helps you when you have gone through hell. You need the courage to continue and not fall back into unhealthy relationships or situations that result in unhealthy cords. Scorpion is here to lend you courage and tenacity. Next, Inchworm and Silkworm appear. Small but mighty, they are here to remind you that no matter how angry or disappointed you may feel, you can take small steps toward healing.

Then you see Butterfly floating through the air. It lands on your nose. Butterfly shows up to remind you that transmuting energy is much more efficient and freeing than constantly battling the cords of connection. You may go through many changes to heal the cords, but once you send forgiveness through them, you are free. Butterfly will even help heal ancestral cording that has gone on for generations. You notice Komodo Dragon approaching. You feel instant relief that Komodo Dragon is here to help you patiently, yet mightily, transmute energy. You feel great confidence in your ability. Finally, Phoenix appears like fire before you. You watch as Phoenix is consumed by flame, turns to ash, and is reborn. You know you are the Phoenix. You are ready.

Once completed, bring your hands together in the middle of your chest in a prayerlike position. Give gratitude for the animal guides that appeared. Ground yourself by feeling the connection from your feet to Mother Earth. You are one with her. Feel energetic roots extending from the bottoms of your feet down into the core of Mother Earth. Wrap the roots around her core and pull some energy back up through your feet and into the rest of your body. Always remember to send some of your gratitude and loving energy through your feet to Mother Earth. Now imagine a place in the cosmos such as a star or a planet. Your higher or soul self may originate from here. Visualize lassoing some of your energy around that star or planet. Give it a little tug. Now you are equally grounded between heaven and earth. When you are ready, bring your attention back into the room and your body. Wiggle your fingers and your toes. When you are ready, slowly and gently open your eyes.

*Chapter Twelve*

# Before I Dazzle You
## *Protective Crystals to Get Started*

Crystals are great tools to help us become superhero transmuters. Crystals work well with us because they have a fixed internal structure and a fixed rate of vibration. We, as humans, have entropy, which is better known as chaos. Our rates of vibration are not fixed; they are ever-changing. When we work with crystals, we entrain to their vibrations. That is why crystals are helpful as tools. There are so many beautiful crystals available and willing to work with us. The ones mentioned in this chapter include lepidolite, selenite, and black kyanite. They are chosen because they have protective qualities that prepare us for the process of transmutation. They will help us learn we are not limited to absorbing, protecting, deflecting, and avoiding energy.

While all of the crystals are helpful and we might want to collect them over time, we need not feel pressure to buy them all. Many are quite affordable, and we may decide to purchase them, but until that time, it will suffice to use a photo of them to visualize their energy. We can even place a photo, such as the photos in this book, beside water and infuse our water with the energy of the photo through our intention. We can also place our feet on the ground and connect to Mother Earth to connect to crystals because, after all, crystals come from Mother Earth. In other words, we can still work with any of these crystals even if we do not own the actual crystal.

After each of the crystals mentioned in this chapter, there is an exercise to connect us to the energy of that crystal to send the properties of the crystal through different cords and to help us on our Superhero's Journey.

## Lepidolite: The Anxiety Buster Crystal

Lepidolite is a way to connect to the violet flame. Lepidolite is a natural source of lithium, which makes it a go-to crystal for those of us suffering from stress, anxiety, panic attacks, or depression. This crystal is recommended for anyone who is an empath. We can use lepidolite to calm us down so that we clearly discern the truth of the matter regarding potentially unhealthy cords. It will also help us inject some of the soothing energy into the cord of connection.

*Exercise*
### Lepidolite

Hold a lepidolite in each of your hands. If you only have one lepidolite, hold it in your receiving hand (nondominant hand). Begin the meditation by looking at the lepidolite in your hands. Notice the purple color of the crystals. Take note of the way the crystals are shaped and any other features of the crystals that are apparent to you. Now close your eyes and draw your attention to your breath. Slow your breathing and calm your mind. Know that these crystals are here to help you transmute energy. Begin to think of your power to transmute energy. You are one with Saint Germain and the violet flame. You are capable of transmuting any energy you desire. Visualize yourself as the violet flame. You are in charge of your energy. You are an alchemist of the most excellent order. Feel yourself calming down. Visualize any concerns melting away. Think only of the soothing lepidolite.

You find yourself in a very safe setting. In this setting, there is nothing but serenity. Everything seems to slow down and soothe you. Your concerns continue to fall away. Your energy will overcome any forces against you. You find beautiful purple items in this safe space, and you begin to become one with all of them. You know that you are vibrating on a higher level each and every time you stand in the flame and become the flame. You are protected and safe. You feel overwhelming peace. You realize you may need to allow yourself to step out of situations that cause you stress or anxiety. You know you can change the form of any energy. You know you can transmute energy for your peace of mind.

When you are ready while holding the lepidolite, bring both hands up to your heart chakra in a prayerlike position. Give gratitude to the lepidolite for soothing you and providing protection during transmutation. Ground yourself by feeling the connection from your feet to Mother Earth. You are one with her. Feel energetic roots extending from the bottoms of your feet down into the core of Mother Earth. Wrap the roots around her core and pull some energy back up through your feet and into the rest of your body. Always remember to send some of your gratitude and loving energy through your feet to Mother Earth. Now imagine a place in the cosmos such as a star or a planet. Your higher or soul self may originate from here. Visualize lassoing some of your energy around that star or planet. Give it a little tug. Now you are equally grounded between heaven and earth. When you are ready, bring your attention back into the room and your body. Wiggle your fingers and your toes. When you are ready, slowly and gently open your eyes.

## Selenite: The Sage Crystal

Selenite is a form of gypsum. Selenite is the perfect stone to rid all layers of our auric field of anything that needs clearing. A long stick of selenite is useful. Like a wand that is used when we go through security at the airport, we stand with our arms and legs apart. Then we wave the selenite wand over our entire auric field. We make sure to clear the bottoms of our feet and our palms just as we would if we were clearing with sage. Once we are cleared, it will help us with sleep and muscle pains. Selenite is the ideal crystal to use when we feel we have absorbed a lot of energy that we have yet to transmute. Not only will it clear the energy, giving us an opportunity to learn to transmute, it will also calm us down. Before we wear selenite or have it near our work areas, we should make sure we can stay awake with this soothing crystal in our auric field.

## *Exercise*
## Selenite

Hold selenite in each of your hands. If you only have one selenite, hold it in your receiving hand (nondominant hand). Begin the meditation by looking at the selenite in your hands. Notice the white color of the crystals. Take note of the way the crystals are shaped and any other features of them that are apparent to you. Now close your eyes and draw your attention to your breath. Slow your breathing and calm your mind. Know that these crystals are here to help you transmute energy.

Begin to visualize your auric field. You realize you have seven layers but begin to visualize the aura as one around your entire body. Examine your aura closely. Is it smooth or does it have indentations or bulbous areas? Are there holes or tears in your aura? Is your aura clear and bright? Is it pale or muddy? Visualize any area that needs smoothing or healing. Visualize the selenite clearing and smoothing any area of your auric field that needs healing. Take your time. You may even want to actually wave the selenite over any areas that you feel need healing.

When you are ready, while holding the selenite bring both hands up to your heart chakra in a prayerlike position. Give gratitude to the selenite for clearing your auric field and providing protection during transmutation. Ground yourself by feeling the connection from your feet to Mother Earth. You are one with her. Feel energetic roots extending from the bottoms of your feet down into the core of Mother Earth. Wrap the roots around her core and pull some energy back up through your feet and into the rest of your body. Always remember to send some of your gratitude and loving energy through your feet to Mother Earth. Now imagine a place in the cosmos such as a star or a planet. Your higher or soul self may originate from here. Visualize lassoing some of your energy around that star or planet. Give it a little tug. Now you are equally grounded between heaven and earth. When you are ready, bring your attention back into the room and your body. Wiggle your fingers and your toes. When you are ready, slowly and gently open your eyes.

## Black Kyanite: The Chakra Balancer Crystal

Black kyanite is an extremely high vibrational stone that looks like a broom or a fan. Because of its shape, it is also known as the witches broom. This high vibrational stone will sweep away perceived negative energy, seal our auras, and clear any effects of psychic or energy vampires. In this context, psychic or energy vampires are beings, human or otherwise, that intentionally suck the life force out of us. As stated in chapter 5, we know that the phrase *energy vampire* may have a different connotation than that of a negative being. If we consider ourselves vampires that sip in toxic energy and recycle it into pure energy, we are transmutation energy vampires.

Black kyanite will also balance our chakras. It is one crystal that I jokingly say could put all other crystals out of business when it comes to balancing chakras. Of course, we can transmute this energy instead if we so desire. That makes us a transmutation energy vampire. We take the energy, transform it, and recycle it into energy for our life force instead of the energy draining our life force.

## *Exercise*
## Black Kyanite

Hold black kyanite in each of your hands. If you only have one black kyanite, hold it in your receiving hand (nondominant hand). Begin the meditation by looking at the black kyanite in your hands. Notice the black color of the broom. Take note of the way the fan is shaped and any other features that are apparent to you. Now close your eyes and draw your attention to your breath. Slow your breathing and calm your mind. Know that these crystals are here to help you transmute energy.

Begin to visualize your chakras. Look at each chakra closely. Begin at the root chakra and go all the way up to your crown chakra. Look at the color of each chakra. Are they gently spinning? Are they overactive and spinning too quickly? Are they underactive and spinning too slowly? Are they healthy and bright in color? Do they seem pale or muddy? Visualize the black kyanite sweeping in a zigzag motion starting at the floor and going over your head. Then reverse the zigzag motion from over your head to the floor. Your chakras will begin to come into balance. Take your time.

When you are ready, while holding the black kyanite bring both hands up to your heart chakra in a prayerlike position. Give gratitude to black kyanite for balancing your chakras, clearing your auric field, and providing protection during transmutation. Ground yourself by feeling the connection from your feet to Mother Earth. You are one with her. Feel energetic roots extending from the bottoms of your feet down into the core of Mother Earth. Wrap the roots around her core and pull some energy back up through your feet and into the rest of your body. Always remember to send some of your gratitude and loving energy through your feet to Mother Earth. Now imagine a place in the cosmos such as a star or a planet. Your higher or soul self may originate from here. Visualize lassoing some of your energy around that star or planet. Give it a little tug. Now you are equally grounded between heaven and earth. When you are ready, bring your attention back into the room and your body. Wiggle your fingers and your toes. When you are ready, slowly and gently open your eyes.

*Chapter Thirteen*

# Bling Me Up

*Crystals for Transmuting Energy*

Crystals are great tools to help us become superhero transmuters. While we will continue to use the crystals in chapter 12, we are ready to begin using crystals for the actual transmutation process. These crystal tools stand prepared to take us to the next level of our ability to change energy. They are also helpful to visually send their properties through our cords of connection. These include red goldstone, blue goldstone, green goldstone, purple goldstone, black tourmaline, black obsidian, Apache tear, amethyst, ametrine, amegreen, and citrine. Remember, while all of the crystals are helpful and we might want to collect them over time, we need not feel pressure to buy these crystals if we do not own them. Many are quite affordable, and we may decide to purchase them, but until that time, a photo of them, such as the photos in this book, will suffice to visualize their energy. We can even place a photo beside water and infuse our water with the energy of the photo through our intention. We can also place our feet on the ground and connect to Mother Earth to connect to crystals. In other words, we can still work with any of these crystals even if we do not own the actual crystal.

After each of the crystals mentioned in this chapter, there is an exercise to connect us to the energy of that crystal to send the properties of the crystal through different cords.

## Goldstone: The Alchemy Crystal

Goldstone is one of the crystals most associated with alchemy and transmutation. Goldstone is a manmade colored glass that looks like it has flecks of glitter. Quartz and silica comprise glass, so goldstone is often called a crystal. Although samples were found in Iran from 1100–1200 CE, the crystal was not called goldstone until later. One version of the lore goes something like this: Goldstone was accidentally created when Italian monks working in a glass factory in the 1600s accidentally tipped copper into a container of glass. It was first called aventurine glass, and finally goldstone. Goldstone was first mentioned in writing when Vincenzo Miotti of Venice was granted the exclusive right to create it.[16]

Not only is goldstone known to deflect energy, it is also an ideal stone to work with when practicing any type of alchemy. Red goldstone contains copper flecks, blue goldstone contains cobalt, green goldstone contains chromium, and purple goldstone contains manganese. Each of these types of goldstone is useful for different types of transmutation. Because of the happenstance creation by the copper falling into the glass, goldstones are ideal for reminding us that there really are no accidents, just opportunities. All too often, we are emotionally, mentally, physically, and spiritually fatigued by the encounter we are attempting to convert; we need strength to begin the transmutation process. All types of goldstone should only be worn or held. Do not use them directly in water or elixirs. Use the indirect or alternative method of infusing. The direct method of infusing with crystals is placing the crystal directly in the water. The indirect, or alternative method, involves placing any crystal that is toxic or water-soluble in a separate and sealed container. The sealed container is then placed in the main water or liquid to infuse it indirectly. Always check the toxicity of all crystals when working with them.

---

16. Hobart M. King, "Goldstone," Geology, accessed May 17, 2020, https://geology.com /gemstones/goldstone/.

## Red Goldstone: The Motivational Crystal

Red goldstone will help us connect to a light source such as the sun's energy for vitality. It will help us turn depressive energy into motivating energy. When we feel so down that we don't think we can transmute energy, red goldstone is the tool we need to help motivate us. It is also ideal for helping us with our sacral chakras if we feel the cord of connection in that area.

*Exercise*
## Red Goldstone

Hold a red goldstone in each of your hands. If you only have one red goldstone, hold it in your receiving hand (nondominant hand). Begin the meditation by looking at the red goldstone in your hands. Notice the beautiful reddish-orange color and the sparkles in the crystals. Take note of the shape of the crystals and any other features of the crystals that are apparent to you. Now close your eyes and draw your attention to your breath. Slow your breathing and calm your mind. Begin to visualize the reddish-orange color of the crystals. See them in your mind's eye. Feel the crystals in your hands. Notice if the crystals feel warm or cold. Do they tingle in your hands? Do they feel light or heavy? Know that these crystals are here to help you transmute energy. The red goldstone will uplift your spirits. Even the slightest boost in your mood or vitality is the transmutation of energy.

When you are ready, draw your attention to any area in your auric field or chakras that may feel discomfort or the source of any cord that may need healing. The red goldstone is often associated with the sacral chakra. It is two finger-widths below your navel. It is the energy center of pleasure, joy, vitality, and creativity. It also connects to any sexual matters. While holding your crystals, draw your hands to this sacral chakra. Hold the crystals there. If you are lying down, you can just place the crystals there if you so desire. Imagine the warmth of the red goldstone going into your sacral chakra. Allow the happy vibration of the red goldstone to lift your spirits. If you feel or sense a cord in the sacral chakra that needs healing, imagine the radiant energy and reddish-orange color of the red goldstone flowing through the cord. Focus only on the cord and the crystals. Let the crystals work for you. Let them help you. Imagine the cord lighting up with the glitter of the crystal. It is glowing and warming up. Keep sending the vibration of this crystal through the cord of connection as long as you feel comfortable doing so.

When you are ready, bring your hands together while holding the crystals in a prayerlike position at your heart chakra. Give gratitude for the transmutation of energy. Ground yourself by feeling the connection from your feet to Mother Earth. You are one with her. Feel energetic roots extending from the bottoms of your feet down into the core of Mother Earth. Wrap the roots around her core and pull some energy back up through your feet and into the rest of your body. Always remember to send some of your gratitude and loving energy through your feet to Mother Earth. Now imagine a place in the cosmos such as a star or a planet. Your higher or soul self may originate from here. Visualize lassoing some of your energy around that star or planet. Give it a little tug. Now you are equally grounded between heaven and earth. When you are ready, bring your attention back into the room and your body. Wiggle your fingers and your toes. When you are ready, slowly and gently open your eyes.

## Blue Goldstone: The Multidimensional Crystal

Blue goldstone is as beautiful as the night sky filled with stars. It will help us pull ourselves into a higher vibration and connect with multidimensional beings that can help us during transmutation. The cobalt in the blue goldstone gives it the property of helping us have strength when we mix energies. When we begin to send energy through a cord that has energy coming from the other end, we realize our light and strength will overcome that of the other energy. Blue goldstone is ideal for this type of difficult transmutation. It will also help us become the witness or observer when working with this type of alchemy. We can visualize ourselves out in the stars. We can anchor to a star so that we become grounded between heaven and earth. As the transmutation is taking place, the blue goldstone, through its work with the throat chakra and third eye, will also help us find our voice, listen, and even feel heard.

## *Exercise*
## Blue Goldstone

Hold a blue goldstone in each of your hands. If you only have one blue goldstone, hold it in your receiving hand (nondominant hand). Begin the meditation by looking at the blue goldstone in your hands. Notice the beautiful, night-sky, color, and the sparkles that look like stars. Take note of the shape of the crystals and any other features of the crystals that are apparent to you. Now close your eyes and draw your attention to your breath. Slow your breathing and calm your mind. Begin to visualize the deep blue color of the crystals. See them in your mind's eye. Feel the crystals in your hands. Notice if the crystals feel warm or cold. Do they tingle in your hands? Do they feel light or heavy? Know that these crystals are here to help you transmute energy.

The blue goldstone helps you pull yourself into a higher vibration and connect with multidimensional beings that can help us during transmutation. Begin to visualize yourself out amongst the stars. Find a star or a planet in the universe. You may even want to anchor to that star or planet so that you become equally grounded between heaven and earth. Begin to think of an energy you wish to transmute. The blue goldstone will begin giving you strength as you think of this transmutation.

This crystal tool is especially helpful when you feel there will be a mixture of energies. If you feel or sense a cord of connection that has energy coming from the other end, you realize the need for your light and strength to overcome that of the other energy. Focus on your blue goldstone to help with this. Allow the blue goldstone to help if it feels as though this is a problematic transmutation. The blue goldstone will help you as you observe from the stars. You can truly become a witness or observer of the alchemy with the help of the blue goldstone. As the transmutation is taking place, place the blue goldstone on your throat chakra and third eye. This placement will help you discern the truth and then be able to speak the truth to yourself, reminding yourself of what truly needs to be released and transmuted. The blue goldstone will then help you find your voice. You will know you can listen to your inner truth and then speak your truth and know your truth is heard.

When you are ready, draw your attention to any area in your auric field or chakras that may feel discomfort, or the source of any cord of connection that may need healing. Imagine the cool blue rays and vibration of the blue goldstone flowing through the cord. Imagine this happening at supersonic speed. The flow is swift, like a rapid river. It is forceful, like the ocean. The powerful light of the blue goldstone overcomes any energy that is flowing toward you through the cord. As it mixes with the energy, potent alchemy takes place. Then the high vibration of the blue goldstone will do its work. Focus only on the cord and the crystals. Let the crystals work for you. Let them help you. Imagine the cord lighting up with the glitter of the crystals. They are glowing so brightly now. Keep sending the vibration of this crystal through the cord as long as you feel comfortable doing so.

When you are ready, bring your hands together while holding the crystals in a prayerlike position at your heart chakra. Give gratitude for the transmutation of energy. Ground yourself by feeling the connection from your feet to Mother Earth. You are one with her. Feel energetic roots extending from the bottoms of your feet down into the core of Mother Earth. Wrap the roots around her core and pull some energy back up through your feet and into the rest of your body. Always remember to send some of your gratitude and loving energy through your feet to Mother Earth. Now imagine a place in the cosmos such as a star or a planet. Your higher or soul self may originate from here. Visualize lassoing some of your energy around that star or planet. Give it a little tug. Now you are equally grounded between heaven and earth. When you are ready, bring your attention back into the room and your body. Wiggle your fingers and your toes. When you are ready, slowly and gently open your eyes.

## Green Goldstone: The Forgiveness from a Distance Crystal

Green goldstone sometimes needs to be taken into the sunlight to recognize its true beauty and worth. Sometimes we are so blind to a situation that we don't realize the damage the unhealthy flow of energy is causing us. We hold onto the attachment, remembering only the good times. We often do this when we have lost our sense of self-worth. Green goldstone will help us find the self-love we need to recognize that the flow of energy is unhealthy. This tool helps us with the process of changing the unhealthy flow through a cord to a stream of love. It will help us trust the process of sending healing light, yet know that it is healthy to move on in forgiveness from a distance.

Chromium is highly resistant to corrosion and tarnishing. For example, stainless steel, which contains chromium, is resistant to tarnishing. The chromium in green goldstone gives it not only the property of helping us polish up the cord, making it shiny again, it also makes it resistant to the corrosive energy that may flow from the other end of the cord. Green goldstone is an ideal stone to work with when we feel the cord of connection at our heart chakra.

## Exercise
### Green Goldstone

Hold a green goldstone in each of your hands. If you only have one green goldstone, hold it in your receiving hand (nondominant hand). Begin the meditation by looking at the green goldstone in your hands. Notice the beautiful green color and the sparkles in the crystals. Take note of the shape of the crystals and any other features of the crystals that are apparent to you. Now close your eyes and draw your attention to your breath. Slow your breathing and calm your mind. Begin to visualize the green color of the crystals. See them in your mind's eye. Feel the crystals in your hands. Notice if the crystals feel warm or cold. Do they tingle in your hands? Do they feel light or heavy? Know that these crystals are here to help you transmute energy. Sometimes we are blinded to the unhealthy flow of energy a cord is causing us. We want to hang onto the attachment even though it may not be healthy for us. Green goldstone is a stone of health. Begin to envision the healing ray of light of the green goldstone.

Allow yourself room to feel self-love; you need to realize that the flow of energy is unhealthy. Ask for a sign of where the cord is connected. If you don't sense an answer, assume it is your heart chakra. Allow the green goldstone to begin changing the unhealthy flow through a cord to a stream of love. Accept the help of the green goldstone and trust the process that healing light is flowing through the cord. Sit in the knowingness that it is healthy to move on in forgiveness from a distance. You do not have to do anything but let the energy transmute in love. The cord will begin to polish up over time. However, once this energy transmutes, the chromium in the green goldstone will make the cord highly resistant to any corrosive energy flowing from the other end. Keep sending the vibration of this crystal through the cord of connection as long as you feel comfortable doing so.

When you are ready, bring your hands together while holding the crystals in a prayerlike position at your heart chakra. Give gratitude for the transmutation of energy. Ground yourself by feeling the connection from your feet to Mother Earth. You are one with her. Feel energetic roots extending from the bottoms of your feet down into the core of Mother Earth. Wrap the roots around her core and pull some energy back up through your feet and into the rest of your body. Always remember to send some of your gratitude and loving energy through your feet to Mother Earth. Now imagine a place in the cosmos such as a star or a planet. Your higher or soul self may originate from here. Visualize lassoing some of your energy around that star or planet. Give it a little tug. Now you are equally grounded between heaven and earth. When you are ready, bring your attention back into the room and your body. Wiggle your fingers and your toes. When you are ready, slowly and gently open your eyes.

## Purple Goldstone: The Higher Consciousness Crystal

Purple goldstone is a rarer goldstone. It is associated with the crown chakra. Use purple goldstone when practicing any of the exercises in this book. The purple goldstone is excellent to use with advanced transmutation. It is connected to the crown chakra and will raise us into higher levels of consciousness with The Collective. It also contains manganese, which has many benefits for physical health.

*Exercise*
## Purple Goldstone

Hold a purple goldstone in each of your hands. If you only have one purple goldstone, hold it in your receiving hand (nondominant hand). Begin the meditation by looking at the purple goldstone in your hands. Notice the beautiful purple color and the sparkles in the crystals. Take note of the shape of the crystals and any other features of the crystals that are apparent to you. Now close your eyes and draw your attention to your breath. Slow your breathing and calm your mind. Begin to visualize the purple color of the crystals. See them in your mind's eye. Feel the crystals in your hands. Notice if the crystals feel warm or cold. Do they tingle in your hands? Do they feel light or heavy? Know that these crystals are here to help you transmute energy.

Begin to think of The Collective. See yourself connected to All That Is. Begin to transmute the energy that comes into your mind. Use beautiful purple goldstone to send high vibration energy through any cord that comes to mind. The Collective needs your help. You are a powerful transmuter. Feel the love healing divisions and discord. Send this energy as far and as wide as you so desire. You will feel yourself growing stronger during this process.

When you are ready, bring your hands together while holding the crystals in a prayerlike position at your heart chakra. Give gratitude for the transmutation of energy. Ground yourself by feeling the connection from your feet to Mother Earth. You are one with her. Feel energetic roots extending from the bottoms of your feet down into the core of Mother Earth. Wrap the roots around her core and pull some energy back up through your feet and into the rest of your body. Always remember to send some of your gratitude and loving energy through your feet to Mother Earth. Now imagine a place in the cosmos such as a star or a planet. Your higher or soul self may originate from here. Visualize lassoing some of your energy around that star or planet. Give it a little tug. Now you are equally grounded between heaven and earth. When you are ready, bring your attention back into the room and your body. Wiggle your fingers and your toes. When you are ready, slowly and gently open your eyes.

## Black Tourmaline (Schorl): The Transmutation Crystal

Black tourmaline, also known as schorl, is known for its ability to not only absorb and deflect energy but also to transmute it. The primary reason black tourmaline is known for its absorption, deflection, and transmutation abilities is that black tourmaline is piezoelectric and pyroelectric. Black tourmaline can generate, accumulate, and store electric charges through piezoelectricity and pyroelectricity. Black tourmaline can absorb and deflect energy we don't want near us. Many do not acknowledge this includes any type of energy. Remember, we label the energy. Most everyone assumes and states that it absorbs only negative energies. But who labels and defines this energy?

Who judges where it is on the spectrum of good and evil? Black tourmaline is capable of absorbing all energies, just as we are. It is up to us to set the intention with the black tourmaline.

In the same way, we scan and identify what cords and energy may need transmuting once we have absorbed the energy. The most important benefit of black tourmaline largely goes underemphasized by many crystal healers, authors, and metaphysical stores—the ability to transmute the absorbed energy. Black tourmaline can change the energy to whatever energy we intend. *Always remember,* black tourmaline is a tool. We are the superheroes, and we also can transmute the energy once we acknowledge our power to do so. Learning to transmute energy is the ultimate way we become the heroes of our own stories and then begin to change the world. We are human black tourmalines.

## *Exercise*
## Black Tourmaline

Hold a black tourmaline in each of your hands. If you only have one black tourmaline, hold it in your receiving hand (nondominant hand). Begin the meditation by looking at the black tourmaline in your hands. Notice the black color of the crystals. Take note of the way the crystals are shaped and any other features of the crystals that are apparent to you. Now close your eyes and draw your attention to your breath. Slow your breathing and calm your mind. Think of the intention you want to set with your black tourmaline. Be very clear about your intention. If you want the black tourmaline to deflect negative energy away from you, set this intention. If you want the crystals to absorb the negativity, set that intention. If you want the black tourmaline to transmute negativity, set that intention.

Once completed, bring your hands together at your heart chakra in a prayerlike position. Give gratitude that the black tourmaline absorbed, deflected, and transmuted energy. Now place the black tourmaline at your feet and allow them to ground you. Feel the energy of the stones pulling toward your feet as you become more and more grounded. Continue to ground yourself by feeling the connection from your feet to Mother Earth. You are one with her. Feel energetic roots extending from the bottoms of your feet down into the core of Mother Earth. Wrap the roots around her core and

AMEGREEN

AMETHYST

AMETRINE

APACHE TEAR

BLACK KYANITE

BLACK OBSIDIAN

BLACK TOURMALINE

BLUE GOLDSTONE

CITRINE

LEPIDOLITE

RED GOLDSTONE

SELENITE

pull some energy back up through your feet and into the rest of your body. Always remember to send some of your gratitude and loving energy through your feet to Mother Earth. Now imagine a place in the cosmos such as a star or a planet. Your higher or soul self may originate from here. Visualize lassoing some of your energy around that star or planet. Give it a little tug. Now you are equally grounded between heaven and earth. When you are ready, bring your attention back into the room and your body. Wiggle your fingers and your toes. When you are ready, slowly and gently open your eyes.

## Black Obsidian: The Shadow Side Crystal

Black obsidian arrowheads have long been used to cut cords. In *The Magic of Connection*, we don't cut cords. We can still work with black obsidian in any shape we choose, but it is important to know what we are dealing with when we do. This amorphous volcanic glass is highly effective for protection, but it should be used in small doses. It can be somewhat harsh in that it may bring up past trauma or issues that we have kept as hidden aspects of ourselves for one reason or another. These shadow sides need to be faced at some point in order to send healing through the cords. But it is very important to be prepared in these situations for what may come up emotionally. If we want to utilize something a little less emotionally jarring, golden sheen obsidian is a gentler form of obsidian that is precisely the energy we want to send through the cords. We want to send a radiant and protective sunlight, yet one that is more soothing. It is much warmer and more conducive to sending light through the cords than regular black obsidian.

### *Exercise*
### Black Obsidian

Hold a black obsidian in each of your hands. If you only have one black obsidian, hold it in your receiving hand (nondominant hand). Begin the meditation by looking at the black obsidian in your hands. Notice the black color of the crystals. Take note of the way the crystals are shaped and any other features of the crystals that are apparent to you. See if you can see images in the reflection of the black obsidian. Now close your eyes and draw your attention to your breath. Slow your breathing and calm your mind. Know that these crystals are here to help you transmute energy. Breathe in deeply and go to the source of your wound. Know that you are protected. Remember to just be the observer of this energy. Pull yourself out of the scene and just look down upon it. Allow yourself to sip in just a little of that which you don't want to see. This is an aspect of you that you keep hidden. It is your shadow side. It also may be something you have pushed far down and feel uncomfortable tapping into at this time. That is perfectly fine. Do not lean into any energy that you are not ready to face and transmute.

If you know the source of the cord, visualize it now. Where do you feel or sense the cord is attached to you? Look at the cord and describe it now. This may be a particularly hideous cord. It is alright; it needs the strong protective energy of the black obsidian sent through the cord. The energy of the black obsidian will fill the cord and begin to transmute the energy flowing through the cord. You will start to see, over time, the cord becomes healthy again. But do not overdo it. Make sure you use your energetic sidekicks as well as any human support you need during this process. Take your time.

When you are ready, bring both hands with the black obsidian up to your heart chakra in a prayerlike position. Give gratitude for the protection and transmutation of the black obsidian. Ground yourself by feeling the connection from your feet to Mother Earth. You are one with her. Feel energetic roots extending from the bottoms of your feet down into the core of Mother Earth. Wrap the roots around her core and pull some energy back up through your feet and into the rest of your body. Always remember to send some of your gratitude and loving energy through your feet to Mother Earth. Now imagine a place in the cosmos such as a star or a planet. Your higher or soul self may originate from here. Visualize lassoing some of your energy around that star or planet. Give it a little tug. Now you are equally grounded between heaven and earth. When you are ready, bring your attention back into the room and your body. Wiggle your fingers and your toes. When you are ready, slowly and gently open your eyes.

## Apache Tear: The Grief Relief Crystal

Apache tear is also a beautiful crystal to use for transmuting energy. Apache tear is another form of obsidian. It is a volcanic glass. However, it is tumbled into a rougher nodule crystal, as opposed to black obsidian, that may be sharper and shinier. Apache tear is named for the tears that were cried as

Native Americans left their lands. The Apache tears were the tears shed. It is especially useful to help us through times of grief. In the throes of grief, it is difficult to operate without a tool. Apache tear helps us go through the stages of grief at the pace that we need to begin our healing process. We are corded to those who transitioned. Many of us know this because we feel, sense, and communicate with our loved ones who are no longer in their earthly bodies. They are still energy beings, and we are corded to them. This awareness gives many of us help in our grieving. Apache tear helps us know that even though we realize our loved one is just in another plane or dimension, it is human to grieve.

Apache tear fires up our connection to Archangel Azrael, who helps us deal with the grief. There are other types of grief, of course. We may have grief from a breakup or grief from the loss of a job. These can cause serious activation of cords. We may have anger, sadness, disappointment, jealousy, or any other uncomfortable energy. For example, when we have a job, we have cords of connection to the job itself, the building, the people, and even the city. Depending on how we leave the job, we will have various cords that may need healing. If we are grieving the loss, Apache tear will help.

*Exercise*
## Apache Tear

Hold an Apache tear in each of your hands. If you only have one Apache tear, hold it in your receiving hand (nondominant hand). Begin the meditation by looking at the Apache tear in your hands. Notice the black color of the crystals. Take note of the way the crystals are shaped and any other features of the crystals that are apparent to you. Now close your eyes and draw your attention to your breath. Slow your breathing and calm your mind. Know that these crystals are here to help you transmute energy. Breathe in deeply and go to the source of your grief. Allow yourself to sit with the grief for as long as you desire. You are most likely aware of the source of your grief, be it the loss of a loved one, a loss of a love relationship, a loss of a job, or any other sort of loss that causes you your grief. You may feel you cannot breathe; the weight is so heavy. Take a deep breath and visualize a weight being taken off of you.

Bring your attention back to the Apache tear in your hands. Realize they are here to help you go through your grief. You can also call upon Archangel Azrael to help you. Ask where the cords are connected. Many times, with grief, they are connected to your heart chakra. Begin to send a soothing pale yellow through the cord. This soothing energy will help you feel the connection in any way that best serves you. If it is something else you are grieving, such as a job that was not for your highest good, still send pale yellow through the cord. This will begin to transform your grief into a knowingness that your highest and best good is tenderly being cared for at this time.

When you are ready, bring both hands with the Apache tear up to a prayerlike position at your heart chakra. Give gratitude for the protection and transmutation of the Apache tear. Ground yourself by feeling the connection from your feet to Mother Earth. You are one with her. Feel energetic roots extending from the bottoms of your feet down into the core of Mother Earth. Wrap the roots around her core and pull some energy back up through your feet and into the rest of your body. Always remember to send some of your gratitude and loving energy through your feet to Mother Earth. Now imagine a place in the cosmos such as a star or a planet. Your higher or soul self may originate from here. Visualize lassoing some of your energy around that star or planet. Give it a little tug. Now you are equally grounded between heaven and earth. When you are ready, bring your attention back into the room and your body. Wiggle your fingers and your toes. When you are ready, slowly and gently open your eyes.

## Purple Crystals: Collectively, The Violet Light Crystals

Saint Germain is an ascended master (sidekick) who helps us transmute energy through his violet light or flame. The violet light or flame is one of transmutation. Several purple crystals are ideal to call on Saint Germain and his violet light. Amethyst, ametrine, and amegreen are all helpful in using the transmutational energy of the violet flame.

## Amethyst: The Transmutation by Fire Crystal

Amethyst is a type of quartz that gets its purple color from color centers (defects) in the quartz. These color centers are created by trace amounts of irradiated iron. It is fascinating that the color comes from a defect in the amplifying and clarifying quartz. Amethyst is loosely translated as the Greek word for *undrunk* or *not intoxicated*. Greek warriors lined their chalices with amethyst to be prepared for battle after a night of drinking their wine. Because of this, amethyst is often recommended for addictive behavior. It also helps with calming, sleeping, and relieving headaches. Purple is associated with the crown chakra and calls in the violet flame.

Many of us are unaware that when amethyst is heated, it turns a burnt orange color and is called citrine. This is transmutation by fire!

## *Exercise*
## Amethyst

Hold an amethyst in each of your hands. If you only have one amethyst, hold it in your receiving hand (nondominant hand). Begin the meditation by looking at the amethyst in your hands. Notice the purple color of the crystals. Take note of the way the crystals are shaped and any other features of the crystals that are apparent to you. Now close your eyes and draw your attention to your breath. Slow your breathing and calm your mind. Know that these crystals are here to help you transmute energy. Begin to think of your power to transmute energy. You are one with Saint Germain and the violet flame. You are capable of transmuting any energy you desire. Visualize yourself as the violet flame.

You are in charge of your energy. You are an alchemist of the most excellent order. The amethyst pulls you into your crown chakra, and you know that you are vibrating on a higher level each and every time you stand in the flame and become the flame. You are protected and safe. But even more, you do not feel as much of a need to feel protected and safe. You know you can change the form of any energy into that which is for your best and highest good. You also know that the element of fire is a quick-acting element. In an instant, you see the results of your transmutation work.

When you are ready, bring both hands with the amethyst up to your heart chakra in a prayerlike position. Give gratitude for the protection and transmutation of the amethyst. Ground yourself by feeling the connection from your feet to Mother Earth. You are one with her. Feel energetic roots extending from the bottoms of your feet down into the core of Mother Earth. Wrap the roots around her core and pull some energy back up through your feet and into the rest of your body. Always remember to send some of your grat-itude and loving energy through your feet to Mother Earth. Now imagine a place in the cosmos such as a star or a planet. Your higher or soul self may originate from here. Visualize lassoing some of your energy around that star or planet. Give it a little tug. Now you are equally grounded between heaven and earth. When you are ready, bring your attention back into the room and your body. Wiggle your fingers and your toes. When you are ready, slowly and gently open your eyes.

## Ametrine: The Higher Power Crystal

Ametrine is a natural combination of amethyst and citrine. It has all the prop-erties of clear quartz, amethyst, and citrine. These properties include, but are not limited to, clarity, amplification, serenity, addiction breaking, cheerfulness, and confidence building. It connects our solar plexus to our crown chakra. It lets us know we are worthy of our connection with Divine. Ametrine is ideal for working on cords where we feel intimidated by the energy of someone else. Perhaps they are a boss or someone we looked up to at some point. The citrine will give us the confidence to begin the cord healing process.

### *Exercise*
### Ametrine

Hold an ametrine in each of your hands. If you only have one ametrine, hold it in your receiving hand (nondominant hand). Begin the meditation by looking at the ametrine in your hands. Notice the purple and orange color of the crystals. Take note of the way the crystals are shaped and any other features of the crystals that are apparent to you. Now close your eyes and draw your attention to your breath. Slow your breathing and calm your mind. Know that these crystals are here to help you transmute energy. Begin to think of your power to transmute energy. You are one with Saint Germain and the violet flame. You are capable of transmuting any energy you desire. Visualize yourself as the violet flame.

You are in charge of your energy. You are an alchemist of the most excep-tional order. Feel yourself growing in confidence. Your energy will overcome any forces against you. You are worthy of every good thing, and you are feel-ing the warmth of the ametrine. The crystals connect your solar plexus with your crown chakra. You feel confident and have more vitality and motivation. You know that you are vibrating on a higher level each and every time you stand in the flame and become the flame. You are protected and safe. You feel less and less intimidated or concerned about any cord that has been worrying you. You begin to know you do not need the help of tools as much to feel protected and safe. You know you can change the form of any energy into that which is for your best and highest good. You also know that the element of fire is a quick-acting element. In an instant, you see the results of your transmutation work.

When you are ready, bring both hands with the ametrine up to your heart chakra in a prayerlike position. Give gratitude for the protection and transmutation of the ametrine. Ground yourself by feeling the connection from your feet to Mother Earth. You are one with her. Feel energetic roots extending from the bottoms of your feet down into the core of Mother Earth. Wrap the roots around her core and pull some energy back up through your feet and into the rest of your body. Always remember to send some of your gratitude and loving energy through your feet to Mother Earth. Now imagine a place in the cosmos such as a star or a planet. Your higher or soul self may originate from here. Visualize lassoing some of your energy around that star or planet. Give it a little tug. Now you are equally grounded between heaven and earth. When you are ready, bring your attention back into the room and your body. Wiggle your fingers and your toes. When you are ready, slowly and gently open your eyes.

## Amegreen: The Higher Love Crystal

Amegreen is a natural combination of amethyst and prasiolite. Prasiolite is green amethyst, and since amethyst is a quartz, amegreen is also known as green quartz. Amegreen has all the properties of quartz, amethyst, and prasiolite. These properties include, but are not limited to, clarity, amplification, serenity, addiction breaking, compassion, and love. It connects our heart chakra to our crown chakra. It reminds us to show love and compassion when transmuting energy. It is perfect to use for cords where our spiritual knowingness encourages us to recycle energy for ourselves and to help Mother Earth.

*Exercise*
## Amegreen

Hold an amegreen in each of your hands. If you only have one amegreen, hold it in your receiving hand (nondominant hand). Begin the meditation by looking at the amegreen in your hands. Notice the purple and green color of the crystals. Take note of the way the crystals are shaped and any other features of the crystals that are apparent to you. Now close your eyes and draw your attention to your breath. Slow your breathing and calm your mind. Know that these crystals are here to help you transmute energy. Begin to think of your power to transmute energy. You are one with Saint Germain and the violet flame. You are capable of transmuting any energy you desire. Visualize yourself as the violet flame. You are in charge of your energy. You are an alchemist of the most excellent order. Feel yourself growing in confidence. Your energy will overcome any forces against you. You are worthy of every good thing, and you are feeling the love of the amegreen. The crystals connect your heart chakra with your crown chakra. You begin to swell up with a love for yourself, others, and The Collective. You know that you are vibrating on a higher level each and every time you stand in the flame and become the flame. You are protected and safe.

You feel overwhelming love. You realize you may need to forgive some people and love them from a distance. You know you can change the form of any energy into that which is for your best and highest good. You know you are here to transmute energy for The Collective. You are capable of holding space and love for so many in The Collective. Your heart is full of loving energy that you may use in any way you desire. You also know that the element of fire is a quick-acting element. In an instant, you see the results of your transmutation work.

When you are ready, bring both hands with the amegreen up to your heart chakra in a prayerlike position. Give gratitude for the protection and transmutation of the amegreen. Ground yourself by feeling the connection from your feet to Mother Earth. You are one with her. Feel energetic roots extending from the bottoms of your feet down into the core of Mother Earth. Wrap the roots around her core and pull some energy back up through your feet and into the rest of your body. Always remember to send some of your gratitude and loving energy through your feet to Mother Earth. Now imagine a place in the cosmos such as a star or a planet. Your higher or soul self may originate from here. Visualize lassoing some of your energy around that star or planet. Give it a little tug. Now you are equally grounded between heaven and earth. When you are ready, bring your attention back into the room and your body. Wiggle your fingers and your toes. When you are ready, slowly and gently open your eyes.

## Citrine: The Clear and Cheer Crystal

Citrine is a form of quartz. It is rarer than other types of quartz. Many of the crystals that we think are citrine are actually created through a man-made process of heat treating amethyst or even smoky quartz. Citrine properties first come from the fact that it is a quartz. All quartz crystals amplify and clarify. They draw our attention to what we need to see and understand. They also amplify situations, so we are forced to deal with them. The orange color of citrine connects to the sacral chakra. Often, it is a light yellow and then relates to the solar plexus. It is a crystal that has undergone transmutation either by earth or by man. This is why it is often known as a crystal that makes us feel warm and happy. It is proof that transmutation works. Citrine helps us have the confidence to begin practicing transmutation, reminding us that we have the power to transmute even difficult cords to healthy cords. It is also useful in healing cords connected in our sacral chakra or solar plexus.

*Exercise*
### Citrine

Hold a citrine in each of your hands. If you only have one citrine, hold it in your receiving hand (nondominant hand). Begin the meditation by looking at the citrine in your hands. Notice the orange color of the crystals. Take note of the way the crystals are shaped and any other features of the crystals that are apparent to you. Now close your eyes and draw your attention to your breath. Slow your breathing and calm your mind. Know that these crystals are here to help you transmute energy. Begin to think of your power to transmute energy. In an instant, you are transported to a warm place full of sunshine. You feel the warmth of the sun on your face.

You are worthy of every good thing, and you are feeling the warmth of the citrine. The crystals are associated with your solar plexus, which is right below your rib cage. It is your power center. You begin to feel confident and have more vitality and motivation. You are protected and safe. You begin to sense any cord of connection that has been worrying you. You realize this attachment may have taken a toll on your sense of self. It may have instilled a feeling of unworthiness. You may feel weak, but the citrine begins to revitalize you so that you can step back into your power. You know you can change the form of any energy into that which is for your best and highest good. You begin to send the warm sunshine energy and light of the citrine through the cord. As you visualize this flow, know that you are becoming stronger and stronger. You are more and more confident. You are in charge of this energy. No one else is. You are managing energy.

When you are ready, bring both hands with the citrine up to your heart chakra in a prayerlike position. Give gratitude for the protection and transmutation of the citrine. Ground yourself by feeling the connection from your feet to Mother Earth. You are one with her. Feel energetic roots extending from the bottoms of your feet down into the core of Mother Earth. Wrap the roots around her core and pull some energy back up through your feet and into the rest of your body. Always remember to send some of your gratitude and loving energy through your feet to Mother Earth. Now imagine a place in the cosmos such as a star or a planet. Your higher or soul self may originate from here. Visualize lassoing some of your energy around that star or planet. Give it a little tug. Now you are equally grounded between heaven and earth. When you are ready, bring your attention back into the room and your body. Wiggle your fingers and your toes. When you are ready, slowly and gently open your eyes.

*Chapter Fourteen*

# We Inhaled

*Herbs, Incense, and Essential Oils for Transmuting Energy*

Herbs, incense, and essential oils are excellent tools and sidekicks for transmuting energy on our Superhero's Journey. These sidekicks have many properties and uses, but one useful property is the triggering of our olfactory nerves. Our sense of smell is the strongest sense we have connecting us to memories. We probably all have a scent that triggers an emotional response in us. For many, it is a smell that takes us back to our childhood. It may trigger happy or sad memories. Because we all have our individual responses to certain smells, we must consider giving ourselves the freedom to decide which scent will help us the most in any given situation. There are many guidelines available for uses of herbs, incense, and essential oils, but we should never underestimate our judgment regarding what works best for us individually.

Anyone who really knows me knows my favorite scent. It is Coppertone sunscreen. Just bottle up that smell and sell it as a perfume, and it will instantly lift my spirits. If it were an herb, incense, or essential oil, it would be the one I would use for joy, happiness, clarity, clearing, and any other high vibration property. I don't need any book of properties to tell me what lifts my mood. I know already. It does not matter what anyone else thinks of the smell and its effect on them. I know the impact it has on me. It may trigger a different response in someone else. That is precisely my point. We respond to energies differently. While it is helpful to have some guidance on which sidekicks we employee to help us, the direction should be just that—guidance, not dogma. Let us be grateful for the wealth of information available to help us understand any of our sidekicks, and let us also grow in the knowingness of our ability to discern what is most helpful to us. It is worth noting that memories are another form of energetic cords that are attached to us. We can use scent sidekicks to help us fire up memory cords that we want to experience. We can also utilize scent sidekicks to heal memories that do not serve us, making those cords dormant if necessary.

Herbs, incense, and essential oils are not just used for triggering memories; they are helpful for purification, protection, manifestation, clearing, intuition, dreams, courage, motivation, concentration, and many more uses. As we work with herbs, incense, or essential oils, we become more familiar with the ones to use in different situations. This need for various scents is especially true when we are preparing to change the form of energy. We approach the need to transmute energy from an energetic, emotional space. There are often steps we need to take to prepare ourselves for transmuting energy in the cords. Not only will we ultimately transmute energy, but we must first attract the energetic state we desire, such as happiness.

Take for example, an argument with a spouse. If it is a minor spat, we typically can transmute that energy by simply walking away and giving each other a little space. But what if it is a more severe issue such as an argument over money spent on credit cards? The severity of the argument and how it is handled involves more interaction and more energy between the spouses. For our example, let us consider if the argument is over one spouse lying about the use of the credit card. This takes the argument to another level. The point is that at each level in the argument, a different type of energy management is needed. When it is just a spat, it takes little energy to walk away, but a sidekick herb or oil that brings joy might be helpful. As we progress to a more involved disagreement, we might need a sidekick herb or oil, such as one for patience, to help us get to the point of transmuting other energy. Once we are in a serious disagreement, many sidekicks may be employed to not only help us transmute the energy of the ultimate issue, but also to give us the strength to do so. Herbs and oils for courage and discernment would be helpful. If, unfortunately, the argument escalates into something that leads us to believe we should not continue in a relationship with our spouse, we would, as we know, still be corded to that spouse. We would eventually need sidekicks, including herbs and oils to help us heal unhealthy cords.

Ultimately, it is important to know that the preparations for transmutation and the actual acts of transmuting energy all may need varying forms of sidekicks to help. Not every situation can be listed, but a few will get us started. We will begin with a general list of herbs, incense, or essential oils that can be utilized for the six basic emotions that may help or inhibit our process of transmutation. We will talk about the six basic emotions in the next section. Then we will list and discuss some of the suggested herbs, incense, and oils to use when we are to the point of actually transmuting the energy.

Interestingly enough, we will not find the word "transmutation" listed in the many indexes of books as one of the properties of herbs, incense, and oils. This exclusion merely accentuates the current lack of emphasis on our ability and need to transmute energy. But never fear, we are changing that; hell, we are transmuting it!

## Herbs, Incense, and Essential Oils for our Six Basic Emotions

These herbs, incense, and essential oils may be utilized as sidekicks to transmute our energy when we don't feel like transmuting anything. We need to check ourselves before attempting to heal any other situation. Once our energy is transmuted, we may also use these sidekicks to transmute other energy, including energy running through cords. When using herbs, we can burn them or use them to dress candles. These herbs do not need to be food grade, as we are not going to consume them in any way. When using incense, we will burn them. When using essential oils, always check the quality of the brand. If we use them on our bodies, therapeutic grade essential oils are required. With a high-quality oil, we can dilute them with a carrier oil such as coconut oil or almond oil and place on our wrists or the bottoms of our feet. If we are unsure of the quality, we will diffuse the oil. While we know we have a wide range of emotions, for simplicity's sake we will cover Ekman's Six Basic Emotions.[17] Almost all emotions fall under these broad categories. Remember, these six broad emotions and corresponding oils can be used to bring us to a place emotionally where we are ready to then transmute. They can also serve as energetic representations of energy needed to flow through cords.

- Happiness (Enjoyment): holy basil, bergamot, marjoram, citrus
- Sadness: St. John's wort, ginseng, saffron, chamomile, lavender
- Fear: Roman chamomile, juniper berry, frankincense, sandalwood, moth-erwort
- Disgust: peppermint, ginger, vetiver, oregano
- Anger: myrrh, sweet orange, dandelion root, rose, skullcap, thyme, ylang-ylang
- Surprise: gardenia, carnation, wintergreen
- General Healing: carnation, eucalyptus, rosemary, geranium, patchouli

## Herbs, Incense, and Essential Oils for Transmutation

The following herbs are commonly used for protection and clearing. While we may recognize many of the following scent tools for their clearing, cleans-ing, and protecting properties, we will use the scent tools for transmutation at this point on our Superhero's Journey. Light the herb and let it burn while envisioning healing energy flowing through the cord. Employ any other side-kicks you feel are necessary. When purchasing herbs, inquiring where they are sourced is always a good idea to ensure that they are ethically, legally, and sustainably grown and harvested.

---

17. Paul Ekman, "An Argument for Basic Emotions," *Cognition and Emotion* 6, no. ¾ (1992), 169–200, http://www.paulekman.com/wp-content/uploads/2013/07/An -Argument-For-Basic-Emotions.pdf.

## WHITE SAGE

White sage has long been used for medicinal purposes. The Romans and the Greeks used sage for its natural healing properties. Dried white sage has been traditionally used by Native Americans for purification ceremonies. Use white sage when the energy flowing through the cord feels like it may come from past lives. Use also when the energy is flowing between family members or ancestors.

## BLACK SAGE (MUGWORT)

Black sage, which we will refer to as mugwort, is also known as dream weed. It is ideal for enhancing visions and dreams. Use mugwort when the energy flowing through the cord feels very thick and heavy. The cord is possibly holding a lot of anger, fear, and rage. It is also ideal for introspection regarding the cord work that needs to take place.

## CEDARWOOD

Cedarwood was used by King Solomon (master magician and transmuter) to build his temple. The Egyptians also used it for embalming. For these reasons and more, it is suitable for all types of transmutation. It is particularly useful for clearing your mind of clutter so that you can connect to your higher self and determine what kind of energy needs to go through the cord. It is highly spiritual and will send divine love and light through the cord. Another situation in which to use cedarwood may involve a cord between ourselves and a spiritual leader, place of worship, cult, or even a religion.

## COPAL

Copal is a tree resin that was popular as a spiritual cleanser amongst the Maya and the Aztecs. It is still used for clearing away negative energy. We will use copal to coat cords like a sticky resin. Copal will send an energy of golden light through the cord and will not let any energy flow back through the cord toward us. It is ideal to use when the cord is making us depressed.

## FRANKINCENSE

Frankincense has been used in spiritual practices and traded for thousands of years. It is a highly magical, high vibration resin used for purifying and cleansing. Use it to lift your mood before attempting to clear a cord. Then allow the high vibration of frankincense to begin to transmute any low vibration in the cord.

## MYRRH

Myrrh has also been used in spiritual practices and traded for thousands of years. It is a highly magical, high vibration resin. Use it for cord work where you feel someone is sending negative energy through the cord at you. Myrrh will overcome the negative energy and transmute it. However, this is work that may require a lot of focused healing.

## SANDALWOOD

The use of sandalwood in temples dates back thousands of years. It was also used as a funeral incense. It is another high vibration energy that can be used to combat lower vibrational entities to which we may have an unhealthy attachment. Sandalwood is one of the fastest ways to heal a cord of connection. If a cord is connected at the brow chakra, sandalwood is ideal to use to send healing through the cord.

## DRAGON'S BLOOD

Dragon's blood is a resin derived from several varieties of trees. This plant resin has been used across the world for thousands of years for purposes ranging from digestive health to cosmetic dye to spiritual use. Dragon's blood will help slow down turmoil and chaos in our minds regarding a situation. It also calms any turbulence or inflamed emotions flowing through the cord.

## EUCALYPTUS

There are hundreds of types of eucalyptus. Many are native to Australia and have learned to adapt to wildfires and regrow. Eucalyptus prevents us from giving energy to any cords that are dormant and should stay that way. Energy flows where attention goes. If we think a situation is over and we begin to think about it, we can use eucalyptus to stop our mind from waking up the dormant energy. If there is a fire, so to speak, in a cord of connection, eucalyptus will help us adapt to the situation.

## VETIVER

Vetiver is an extremely hardy bunchgrass. Its deep root system makes it helpful for erosion control. In the same way, vetiver helps us with deep cords of connection that need healing. They may have gone unnoticed, yet they are making an impact in our life on some subconscious level. Vetiver helps us discern where a cord is attached to us so that we may begin the process of healing. Vetiver encourages us to stay vigilant in our transmutation of the cord.

The following three exercises use scent or aromatherapy to help either prepare emotionally to transmute energy or to proceed to transmute energy.

### *Exercise*
### Transmutation with Your Favorite Scent

This exercise is to demonstrate the powerful connection scent has to your emotions. You can use these steps to put yourself in the mindset to begin the process of transmutation.

1. What is your favorite smell?

2. What emotion does this smell evoke in you?

3. Is your favorite smell connected to a memory?

4. What are the ways you can use your favorite fragrance as a sidekick in transmutation?

5. Give your favorite scent a symbol for the times you don't have access to the actual scent. Using this symbol will trigger your brain to utilize this scent.

*Exercise*
## Herbs, Incense, and Essential Oils
## for Transmutation Preparation

While similar to your own personal scent, the steps in this exercise help you use herbs, incense, and essential oils for the transmutation of energy. Herbs and incense should be burned. The essential oils may be diffused or worn on the wrists or bottoms of feet.

1. Identify what emotion you are struggling with that is inhibiting your ability to transmute.
2. Write down the emotion you personally need to transmute.
3. Set your intention to transmute this energy.
4. Burn the corresponding herb or incense while wearing the complimentary essential oil on your wrist or feet, or diffusing it.
5. Proceed with transmuting the cords when you feel these sidekicks have helped with the emotion.

*Exercise*
## Herbs, Incense, and Essential Oils for Cord Transmutation

Now that you have managed your energy, you can use this exercise to begin transmutation.

1. Identify the cord you want to heal.
2. Choose a corresponding herb, incense, or essential oil.
3. Burn the herb or incense while visualizing healing going through the cord.
4. Wear the essential oil or diffuse it while envisioning healing going through the cord.
5. Use the herbs, incense, or essential oils in conjunction with any of the exercises and steps for cord healing and transmutation in this book.

*Chapter Fifteen*

# We Are the Fire
## Candles and Spells for Transmutation

C andles are perfect tools to use for transmutation because fire is the element of transmutation. Fire is fast-acting and is also the element of
purification. Candles are perfect to use as sidekicks to help us in our superhero mission to change the energy of this world to one of love. We want to
make sure that we use our superhero powers to elevate and evolve the energy.

There are many superb books available on the use of candles. However,
we want to focus specifically on the use of candles for the transmutation of
energy. This use could include using a single candle to represent the type of
transmutation we want to take place within the cords of connection. We need
to remember all of these candles could also be used to exacerbate a cord in a
way that would not be healing. Our intentions must be very clear. If we have
strong emotions that we need to transmute, we must make sure that we do our
own work before engaging in this candle work involving cords. We should only
transmute energy between cords to promote growth and development to help
someone or something on its evolutionary path.

Following is a list of possible color choices for transmutation and cord work based on my personal experience with cord work, candle work, and archangels:

## GREEN

Green sends healing, balance, nurturing, and love through the cord. Green is a perfect go-to for any type of cord healing. If you can't think of another color to use, it is one that would work for any kind of healing. Green is the color associated with Archangel Raphael, the archangel of healing whose aura is emerald green. Green is also associated with the heart chakra where astral cords typically connect.

## RED

Red acts quickly to send love through the cord. Red is robust and fast-acting energy. For transmutation within cords, this is used to reconnect willing cords on both ends. It will also increase passion. For example, use this for a cord of connection between two consenting people that wish to renew their passion for one another. Red is ideal for a couple reconciling. Red is also associated with the root chakra where cords involving the etheric layer represent our physical body connection regarding feelings of security, safety, and groundedness.

## PINK

Pink works to send compassionate love through the cords. It also sends calming energy for emotions. Pink energy is ideal for friendship or family relationship cords that need healing. The color pink is often associated with the heart chakra, where astral cords typically connect. Archangel Ariel has a pink aura and is the patron angel of animals; therefore, pink is ideal for cords with animals. Grab a pink candle when there is a cord that weighs you down because you feel burdened by it and need to lighten up.

## BLUE

Blue sends tranquility and peace through cords. It can also bring a clearer perception through the cord, helping one or both ends of the cord see things more clearly. It opens a path to better communication. Blue will also facilitate a meeting of the minds. Many times, we think we see things from another's viewpoint when we really don't. Blue helps bring about the flow of mediation and understanding through the cord. This flow of understanding is why blue is useful in any cording we have due to a court case. Blue is also associated with the throat chakra, tied to the etheric template of our auric field. The etheric template includes the entire blueprint for the physical plane, including our personality, identity, and energy. The etheric template connects to our throat chakra—the energy center for speaking our truth, feeling heard, and listening. Because a rich blue is associated with Archangel Zadkiel, use a dark blue candle when forgiveness is needed between cords. Turquoise or teal is associated with Archangel Sandalphon, so those colors of candles are ideal when aggression or anger needs diffusing in cords. Archangel Haniel is associated with a pale blue. Use a pale blue candle when needing to bring about healing over heartbreak.

## ORANGE

Orange brings vitality, cheerfulness, and happiness through cords. It also brings in a decisiveness that may be needed on one or both ends of the cord. Orange corresponds to the second layer of our auric field, which is our emotional body. This layer represents our feelings and emotions and connects to our sacral chakra. Our sacral chakra is the energetic field related to pleasure, creativity, and passion. Archangel Gabriel's aura is copper or orange. Use a copper or orange candle when healing any cord due to communication issues or issues between parents and children.

## YELLOW

Yellow helps with the flow of thoughts and communication through the cord. Yellow will also send a vibration of confidence through the cord. Yellow connects to the third layer of our auric field, which is our mental body. The mental body represents our thoughts, mind, and cognition. It connects to our solar plexus, which is our power center of self-worth. Archangel Azrael has a pale yellow aura, so this color candle is perfect for any cord heading involving any type of grief or loss.

## INDIGO

Indigo will help the energy of wisdom flow through the cord. It will also bring us awareness of other energy, providing a stream of discerning energy in the cord. Indigo connects to the sixth layer, which is our celestial body. The celestial body represents our connection to Source and other beings. It has a stable vibration associated with unconditional love and a feeling of oneness. The celestial body connects to the brow chakra or third eye, our energetic center of intuition and discernment. Indigo is a combination of blue and violet. This combination is the color of Archangel Michael's aura. Michael is a strong protector. When you feel you need any type of protection surrounding a cord issue, use an indigo candle.

## VIOLET

Violet will send spiritual awareness and higher, hidden knowledge through the cord. It can also be used to send tension relief and relaxation through the cord. Violet or purple connects to the seventh layer, which is the ketheric template. It is furthest away from the physical body. It represents oneness with All and vibrates at the highest frequency. It connects to the crown chakra, which is our energetic center of spirituality and enlightenment. Archangel Jeremiel's aura is violet or purple. Use a purple candle for forgiveness and high vibration flowing through cords.

## BROWN

Brown is perfect to use when grounding and stability need to flow through the cord. It is also ideal when the cord involves a connection to the earth or one of the earth's beings, such as land or tree. It would also be an excellent color to represent a city.

## WHITE

White is an all-around candle color for any type of cord healing work. It is perfect when you don't have another color candle or you just can't decide which color to use. It also can be used to send purification, serenity, and peace through the cord. It can be used for cords of new beginnings where any type of relationship has been destroyed and restoration is sought. White is also the color to use when we would like the higher selves represented by the two cord ends to communicate with one another. Archangel Raziel's aura is all the colors of the rainbow. Use a white candle to represent Raziel when healing cords of karmic residue.

## BLACK

Black coats the cord in protection until you feel strong enough to transmute the energy totally. Archangel Michael is the primary archangel for protection. Since black candles are strongly associated with protection, when you want to send strong protection through a cord, black will also connect you to Archangel Michael.

## SILVER

Silver brings brightness to the cord. It shines a light on all areas that need healing. Silver brings in astral healing and is the best color for moon healing. Moon healing and the color silver are often associated with Archangel Haniel. Because Haniel is associated with clear knowing and clear seeing, use a silver candle to help with seeing cord situations as they truly are.

## GOLD

Gold brings warmth and strength like the sun to the cord. It works for the mutual benefit of both ends of the cord. Archangel Michael has gold associated with his aura; therefore, a gold candle is ideal for healing. It brings in the light sword of Michael that sends powerful healing and protection through cords.

The following two exercises utilize candles and spellwork to set an intention for the transmutation of energy.

*Exercise*
## Candle Spell for Healing of Cords

This spell helps you transmute energy by utilizing candles as tools to help with your intention.

Items needed:

- 1 chime candle of any color to represent you (chime candles are about four inches long)
- 1 chime candle of any color to represent the other end of the cord (person, place, situation)
- 1 chime candle of any color to represent the healing and transmutation through the cord
- Optional: 1 black chime candle to represent protection
- Optional: Dressing for candle 3 (candle for healing and transmutation). Any oils or herbs that are mentioned in chapter 14 may be chosen to enhance the energy work. After carving your intentions in candle 3, apply a liberal coat of your chosen essential oil to the candle. Then apply herbs to the candle by rolling the candle in the herbs. Adding oils and herbs to this candle may possibly make it burn more quickly than the other candles. Always use caution when working with fire.

Directions:

Take the candle that represents you (candle 1) and carve your name in it. Set it to your left. Take the candle that represents the other energy (candle 2) and carve the name or situation in the candle. Set it to the right side about twenty inches from the first candle. Take candle 3 and carve your transmutation intention into the candle. Place the third candle halfway between the first two candles. If you choose to use a black candle of protection, place it next to candle 1. State your transmutation three times. Light candles 1 through 4 in order. Set your intention and let the candles burn until they burn out. Setting your intention and letting the candles burn performs the transmutation. You may stand watch or go about your business, but have the transmutation in the forefront of your thoughts. Typically, chime candles burn out within an hour. If the candles have not completely burned themselves out within an hour, snuff them out. Blowing them out tends to scatter the energy. Repeat the next day. Repeat daily until the candles have burned out. For safety purposes, do not leave the burning candles unattended.

This spell will bring more attention to the cord, but your focus is already there, or you wouldn't be thinking of the transmutation process. Just be sure your intentions are for healing the cord. This not only is a powerful representation of the energy flowing through the cords but is also the power of transmutation by fire.

*Exercise*
## Container Spell to Transmute Energy

This spell helps you transmute energy by utilizing tools such as crystals, herbs, and candles to help with your intention. The container represents the transmutation process.

Items needed:

- Container: glass bottle or a clear glass Christmas ornament
- Parchment paper
- Pencil
- Mugwort stick
- 2 pinches of loose mugwort
- Pinch of sea salt (more if desired)
- Black chime candle
- Silver chime candle
- 2 holders for chime candles
- Black tourmaline—small enough to fit inside the opening of the container
- Clear quartz point—small enough to fit inside the opening of the container
- Matches

Directions:

Begin to burn the stick of mugwort to purify you, your space, tools, and container. Turn the container upside down, allowing the smoke of the mugwort to go inside the container.

Write down what you want to transmute on parchment paper with your pencil. Place one pinch of loose mugwort on the paper, saving a pinch for later, and roll up the paper. The mugwort will help with the transmutation and help you connect to the intention. It really doesn't matter if you roll it toward you or away from you because either way, you are changing the energy, not just drawing it toward you or away from you. Place it inside the container.

Next, add a black tourmaline to the container. This represents the absorption and transmutation that you are as a human black tourmaline. Next, add the clear quartz point for amplification. Then add the desired amount of sea salt for purification.

Set the bottle to the side. Place the silver chime candle to the right of the container at least two inches away. Repeat your intention or incantation three times as you are lighting the silver candle.

Seal the container with a cork or lid. Now light the black chime candle and use the melting wax to seal the top of your glass container. Sprinkle the other pinch of mugwort into the melting wax on top of the container. Next, place the black chime candle in the melting wax and let it continue to melt, sealing the container. Let both candles continue to burn and let the magic occur. Once the spell has done its work, you may reuse the bottle and the crystals. Just make sure you burn the parchment paper. If you don't wish to keep the container, just release with love and gratitude before disposal.

*Chapter Sixteen*

# It's a Fool's Journey
## *Tarot for Transmuting Energy*

Tarot is a divination tool traditionally comprised of a deck consisting of seventy-eight cards with twenty-two major arcana and fifty-six minor arcana. The major arcana cards are known as The Fool's Journey. The journey is a representation of the process of transmutation from start to finish, much like our Superhero's Journey. Therefore, any of the major cards could be utilized at some point in our process. Each card has a specific meaning but can also be subject to intuitive interpretation. There are also positions assigned to the cards called spreads. Each position within a spread has a special meaning. The divination all comes together when the meaning of the card is combined with the meaning of the card's position in the spread in order to impart information. It is a great tool to use for transmutation.

Tarot connects us to the collective unconscious. The collective unconscious is a phrase coined by Carl Jung that refers to the deepest part of our psyche that is shared with everyone. Due to the extensiveness with which tarot has been used and the underlying structure of the tarot, including archetypes, tarot represents—and is a tool to access—The Collective. When we get our conscious mind out of the way, we can begin to tap into The Collective using tarot. Once we tap into The Collective, tarot can be used to help us heal cords of connection to strengthen the bond between us all. We can work with tarot as one of our sidekicks. We can read tarot to give us insight into our cords of connection, but we can also visualize the cards as sidekicks to guide us through the transmutation process. The more we work with the cards, the more they come alive for us.

## Cards to Help with Transmutation

While there are seventy-eight tarot cards, there are certain cards that specifically relate to transmutation of energy. These archetypal energies are not only utilized in tarot spreads, but they also may serve as sidekicks on our Superhero's Journey.

### THE FOOL

The Fool is a great companion to get us started on our transmutation journey. The Fool helps us know we do not have to be perfect to begin. We just need to start. That is the beauty of changing energy. It happens reasonably quickly once we just take the leap of faith. We will experience all sorts of new beginnings once we start to transmute energy. There is no limit to the journey. However, we do want to make sure we practice. We never want to become careless with energy. We must manage our energy at all times.

### THE MAGICIAN

The Magician is the alchemist. Transmuting energy is the job of The Magician. The Magician provides us with all the tools we need for the transmutation process. We only need to trust our ability to apply the tools correctly when required. The Magician will help us have the confidence to move forward on our transmutation journey. Intellect and decision-making ability will also become enhanced when working with The Magician.

### THE HIGH PRIESTESS

While The Magician gives us practical tools for transmutation, The High Priestess provides us with any hidden knowledge we need to work on cords connecting us with other energy. There may be certain things about the cords that we need revealed to us, such as where the cord is attached to our energy field or auric field. The High Priestess will help us intuitively find and identify any attachments that need healing.

## THE HANGED MAN

The Hanged Man represents transformation and transmutation. We may take a hiatus to gain clarity regarding a cord in our lives. Perhaps we need to see things from a completely different perspective to gain insight into the situation. Once we slow down and examine the cord, we will gain wisdom and a spiritual perspective regarding the flow of energy through the cord. Our change in perspective has already begun the transmutation process. We will continue the process as we send healing through the cords.

## DEATH

The Death card will help bring about the transformation and transmutation. We know that we will remain corded, but we also know there is a need for rebirth and positive change. We can work with Death when we know we need to bring about change, but we are hesitant to do so. We can also work with Death when a change is forced upon us that leaves us in despair. Death will help us know how to heal the cord so that we can see and experience the new opportunities and renewal that are waiting for us.

## TEMPERANCE

Temperance is a card of alchemy and transmutation. It involves the blending and mixing of different energies to achieve balance. Many times, we have cord situations where we simply feel we are the opposite of someone or are completely misunderstood. Often, we are just saying the same thing in different ways. This is an excellent time to work with Temperance as a sidekick. Another situation is when we are corded to someone in a different dimension than us, such as a loved one who has crossed. Temperance can help us work through any cords that need healing with someone in a different dimension.

## THE TOWER

The Tower may be a sidekick that we are hesitant to call on for help, but may be one of the most helpful in the long run. When we resist healing energetic bonds because we are afraid of the change that the healing will bring, The Tower is the sidekick we need. Sometimes we are so obstinate to the change we need that The Tower may come into our lives because our higher self knows it will get us to make the necessary changes that will ultimately put us in a better situation. Either way, we can work with The Tower to help move us through changes during our transformation process that may feel very difficult but will ultimately lead to empowerment in our lives.

## THE WORLD
The World is our sidekick of affirmation, always reminding us that we are in charge of the energy and we can heal any cords, ties, chains, or strongholds in our lives. We have the power. We can complete the transmutation process and experience the liberation of having changed the energy.

## THE MINOR ARCANA
The minor arcana are cards that can represent different stages in our transmutation process and represent specific experiences and situations with cords of connection.

## EIGHT OF WANDS
The Eight of Wands is a great sidekick to represent swift action flowing and traveling through the cords. The fire of the wands represents taking action and is symbolic of the cords firing up with healing very quickly.

## TEN OF SWORDS
The Ten of Swords is an ideal sidekick when we feel in great despair and face a great abyss. Once we face the abyss, we can send swift healing through the cords to transmute the energy into newness of life, but it is often difficult and painful.

---

In the following two exercises, pay close attention if one of the tarot transmutation sidekicks appears in the spread or the card layout. The appearance of a transmutation sidekick alerts us to an added emphasis to the card's message.

## *Exercise*
## The Magic of Connection Tarot Spread

This spread can be used broadly for any type of cording issue. It allows you to understand the energy involved, the source of the energy, and any needed healing. Pay close attention if one of the tarot transmutation sidekicks appears in the spread or the card layout. The appearance of a transmutation sidekick alerts us to an added emphasis to the card's message.

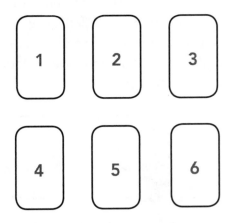

*Figure 4: The Magic of Connection Tarot Spread*

Items needed: Any full tarot deck

- Card 1: What is the issue you want to transmute?
- Card 2: What or who is the source of this issue?
- Card 3: Where is the cord attached? Special note: this could be anywhere in the body or auric field.
- Card 4: What type of energy are you sending through the cord?
- Card 5: What type of energy is the source of the issue sending through the cord? Special note: the cord's source may not be sending any energy or may be neutral in their energy.
- Card 6: What should you do to heal the cord of connection?

## *Exercise*
## Transmutation Tarot Spread

This spread can be used in two ways. The first way is to determine where you are at any given time on your Superhero's Journey. This determination of where you are on your journey (a journey read) helps you to reflect on each level in your cyclical journey. This spread is useful throughout your journey because you know your growth is multidimensional and nonlinear. The second way to use this spread is for specific situations (a situation read). Each card will help you assess the energy you are absorbing, deflecting, or transmuting. Pay close attention if one of the tarot transmutation sidekicks appears in the spread or the card layout. The appearance of a transmutation sidekick alerts us to an added emphasis to the card's message.

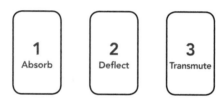

*Figure 5: Transmutation Tarot Spread*

Items needed: Any full tarot deck

- Absorb (Unequipped Empath): On a journey read, the first (left) card represents how you approach handling energy. In a situation read, the first (left) card represents what you need to know about the energy you have absorbed.

- Deflect (Empath in Training): On a journey read, the second (middle) card represents how you approach handling energy. In a situation read, the second (middle) card represents what you need to know about deflecting energy.

- Transmute (Equipped Empath): On a journey read, the third (right) card represents how you approach handling energy. In a situation read, the third (right) card represents what you need to know about transmuting energy.

## *Exercise*
## Circle of One Through Tarot

This exercise is impactful because it helps you understand many important concepts. It helps you realize we are all connected energy that forms a
oneness known as The Collective, which is connected to Source. The power
of this exercise comes from the small-scale model of the group represent-
ing The Collective. Additionally, this exercise deepens your connection with
your tarot tool and encourages you to examine the footprint you are leaving
on Mother Earth.

### Instructions for Preparation

Estimate the number of participants. Ideally, have at least four. Purchase at
least that many index cards in three different colors making sure there is one
of each color for each participant. For each of the three colors, number them
from one through the number of participants. Then write the following three
questions on the index cards, one question per card.

1. What is a struggle you survived or overcame that you use or could use
   to help others?
2. What is your greatest accomplishment, and how does it make the
   world a better place?
3. What is something specific that you want to do for this world? (The
   footprint you want to leave). Next, cut yarn about two feet long and
   staple random, evenly spaced tarot cards to the yarn.

### Instructions for Each Participant:

As you begin the activity, grab three different colored index cards that are
pre-numbered, and have the three questions pre-written on them. Randomly
draw a piece of yarn that already has three tarot cards affixed to it (left, middle, right). Look at your index cards and assign one index card to each of the
three tarot cards. Paper clip the index card to the backside of the tarot card.
Spend time reflecting on the connections and insights between the cards and
questions.

## Instructions for The Collective:

Sit in chairs in a circle, preferably by someone you don't know. To symbolize the concept of oneness, hold your yarn stretched out in both hands up in the air. Notice the circle formed around the room, demonstrating the oneness of all.

## Discussion Time:

First, appoint a facilitator. The facilitator numbers off people sitting next to one another in pairs. The pairs discuss their tarot cards and their corresponding index cards. Each takes three minutes to share both of their cards for a total of six minutes. Next, ask the pair to find correlations and connections in their cards. The partnership discusses any connections or similarities. Next, turn to the person on the left and repeat for another six minutes. Finally, the entire group shares insights from their discussions for the remaining time. The facilitator can note and highlight any additional observations that emphasize the concepts of oneness, The Collective, and our connection to Source. Participants are encouraged to keep their yarn with tarot and index cards.

Special Note: This exercise can be completed individually if the participant does not have access to a group or simply wants to gain more in-depth insight into tarot as a tool.

*Chapter Seventeen*

# Work It

## *Transmutation in Action*

Congratulations! We have accepted our call to adventure. Our world needs superheroes to change the course of cosmic history. We know that we absorb energy and are needed to mold that energy for the highest good. No one is telling us it will be easy. It isn't a small calling. Yet we have accepted our call to adventure—our call to action. We realize that many will refuse this call. We place no judgment on them. We merely step forward in our calling. *The Magic of Connection* has provided us with tools, exercises, and sidekicks to help us on our journey.

Many of us began as Level One Unequipped Empaths. We often suffered consequences of absorbing energy because we were unaware of how to utilize protection. We faced trials such as hearing we were too sensitive or too weak. At this level, we chose to believe it. We were tempted to stick to the status quo to remain safe; however, we ultimately accepted the invitation to face our worst fears. We began to realize that to continue on our Superhero's

Journey, we needed the training to handle our energy. We needed protection from all the energy we absorbed.

Once we realized we absorbed energy, we entered as a Level Two Empath in Training. At this level on our Superhero's Journey, we learned to deflect energy mindfully. A lot of practice took place when we were in training to become masters of our energy. We learned tools of protection such as bubbles, eggs, shields, mirrors, walls, and invisibility suits to help us face trials where energy was thrown at us that we were not ready to handle. We also became familiar with sidekicks and tools such as affirmations, mantras, meditations, spirit guides, animal guides, herbs, incense, essential oils, candles, spells, and tarot. These provide protection and deflection from unwanted energy. We realized and acknowledged that many of us still needed practice reframing our thinking around not only labeling energy but also managing it. We also realized we still absorbed energy even with protective measures. We also began to understand we could choose what to do with that energy. We began to realize we could sip energy. Perhaps it took many moments of sipping in tiny amounts of difficult energy so that we could begin our practice of transmutation.

At that point, we may have had a crisis or a dark night of the soul. We had to make a decision whether or not we wanted to step into the fullness of our Superhero's Journey. We then had to decide if we were going to continue in defensive mode using protection tools only, or if we wanted to become the superhero we were meant to be and transmute energy.

Finally, we reached and implemented the critical level that had been ignored. We became Level Three Equipped Empaths and learned to transmute energy. We embarked on simple situations such as someone cutting us off in traffic, then eventually progressed to seemingly harder types of transmutation. The truth is that all sorts of transmutation are unquestionably the same. It is because we have assigned emotional labels to certain situations that seem harder than others. We began welcoming the energy that was so sloppily thrown around by humans and other beings. We consumed with intention. We knowingly and fearlessly breathed in even so-called negative energy and transmuted it.

Once we know we can transmute energy, we then begin turning that energy into power for ourselves so we can help a world in need. We help others by showing compassion to the underdogs, uplifting the downtrodden, recognizing the fellow empaths in need of assistance, sensing the fear behind those who are wreaking havoc in the world, and bringing together those of us who feel disconnected by living a life that shows the world we are indeed all one. We do this emotion by emotion. Relationship by relationship. Cord by cord. This is our Superhero's Journey.

It might behoove us to reassess our journey. Where are we now? The following exercise is the same that was presented at the beginning of our journey.

## *Exercise*
## Where Am I on My Superhero's Journey? (Take Two)

This exercise will help you assess where you are on your Superhero's Journey.

Assess where you are on your Superhero's Journey by rating the following fifteen statements. Be honest in your assessment, realizing that you never remain in the same place on your journey. The journey is cyclical. While you might be quite evolved in some parts of your journey, you might need improvement in other areas. Transmutation takes practice and diligence. Return to this self-assessment any time you want to assess your energy. It also helps to journal regarding opportunities for improvement and what situations might trigger regression.

(Scoring: Scale from 1-5. Never = 1, Seldom = 2, Sometimes = 3, Often = 4, Always = 5)

1. I am overwhelmed in social situations.
2. I have anxiety, and it keeps me from doing things.
3. I put others ahead of myself to my detriment.
4. I self-sabotage.
5. I am affected by people's energy.
6. I take on the burdens of others.
7. I can't watch or read anything violent.
8. I care for others at the expense of myself.
9. I can't be around anything that triggers past traumatic events.
10. I worry what other people think of me.

11. I mentally replay things I have said or done.

12. I dim my light instead of allowing myself to shine.

13. I dim my light instead of allowing myself to shine.

14. I feel drained after events.

15. I let energy affect me.

Scoring Results: Tally your total score. If you scored 15 to 30, you are currently operating at the Equipped Empath level. If you scored 31 to 52, you are currently operating at the Empath in Training level. If you scored 53 to 75, you are currently operating at the Unequipped Empath level. Remember, our journey is not linear; it is cyclical. We are multidimensional beings. No level is better or worse than the other. Just let it guide you, not label you. Allow yourself to be in the energy of the journey.

*Exercise*
## The Magic of Connection Healing

This exercise weaves together *The Magic of Connection* in one final exercise.

Use this exercise to bring together all the concepts, tools, and sidekicks into one final magical exercise of connection to heal cords. As you complete each step, write your thoughts and insights on the worksheet. There are a few things to remember. First, although it is helpful, you do not actually have to use the tangible tools. Using a photo or visualizing them is sufficient.

*Part One: The Superhero's Call to Adventure*

This section aims to set us on our superhero's path to discover what cords are an issue and need healing.

1. Perform an Empath Energy Scan to check your own energy. Refer to chapter 2.

2. Set your intentions utilizing your tools of affirmations, mantras, and meditations. Refer to chapter 9.

3. Choose any crystals from chapter 12 you'd like to use for protection.

4. Choose any protective tools from chapter 4 of the book, such as bubbles or shields.

5. Utilize one of the following exercises to help you realize what work needs to occur in the cords: Recognizing Different Cord Encounters or Healing Dysfunctional Cords. Refer to chapter 5.

6. Utilize a tarot sidekick by working with *The Magic of Connection* tarot spread. Let your tarot sidekick give you direction in your cord healing. This will help you know what specific sidekicks and tools are needed. Refer to chapter 16.

7. Work through any of the exercises in this book with your team. Also, remember this cord work will change with various cord healings. We are all connected, but each situation is unique.

*Part Two:*
The purpose of this section is to ascertain the specific tools and sidekicks you need for this cord healing. You may end up using one or all of these tools and sidekicks.

1. Pick a guide from chapter 10 based on the cord work that you determined is needed.

2. Pick an animal guide from chapter 11 based on the cord work that you determined is needed.

3. Pick a transmutation crystal from chapter 13 based on the cord work that you determined is needed.

4. Pick herbs, incense, or essential oils from chapter 14 based on the cord work that you determined is needed.

5. Pick a candle or spell from chapter 15 based on the cord work that you determined is needed.

6. Pick a tarot sidekick from chapter 16 based on the cord work that you determined is needed.

*Exercise*
## The Magic of Connection: Worksheet
*Part One: The Superhero's Call to Adventure*
The purpose of this section is to discover what cords are an issue and need healing.

1.  Empath Energy Scan results:    _____

2.  Affirmation: I can    _____

    Mantra: I can    _____

    Meditation:    _____

3.  Protective crystals:    _____

4.  Tools of protection from chapter 4:    _____

5.  Insights from exercises from chapter 5:    _____

6.  *The Magic of Connection* Tarot Spread: Cards 1-6 and any impressions or interpretations that came from the associated questions.

    Card 1:    _____

    Card 2:    _____

    Card 3:    _____

    Card 4:    _____

    Card 5:    _____

    Card 6:    _____

7.  Discoveries from other exercises:    _____

*Part Two: The Superhero's Tools and Sidekicks*

The purpose of this section is to home in on the specific tools and sidekicks you need for this cord healing. You may end up using one or all of these tools and sidekicks.

1.  Guides:    _____

2.  Animal guides:    _____

3.  Transmutation crystals:    _____

4.  Herbs:    _____

    Incense:    _____

    Essential oils:    _____

5.  Candles or spells:    _____

6.  Tarot sidekicks:    _____

Once you have recorded everything you need for the cord work, you may choose to sit or lie down surrounded by these tools and sidekicks as representations of the energy you want to send through the cord in order to bring about healing. Use any or all of the exercises you learned in part one of this book to visualize the healing energy going through the cord. If you want a visual reminder to keep the energy flowing, you can add a personal altar or special area in your home with these items to represent *The Magic of Connection*. Remember that you are the superhero in your journey of transmutation.

# Note to the Reader

My hope is that you will realize you are magical. The next time someone underestimates you, tells you that you are too sensitive, targets you for your success, or hurts you to your core, please remember they are attacking some part of themselves. After all, we are all one. Inwardly, thank them for the opportunity to transmute energy. I know this is not easy, but your ability to transmute will ultimately benefit all involved.

Learn to embrace the heights of hope instead of bracing for the depths of despair. You have the power to change the world. Be the ripple that starts the wave. Put on your cape of compassion and become the superhero this hurting world needs. Heal cords rather than cutting them. Then you will truly experience *The Magic of Connection* and bring the healing needed to this world in pain.

# Bibliography

"Einstein Explains the Equivalence of Energy and Matter." The Center for History of Physics. Transcribed from *Atomic Physics*. J. Arthur Rank Organization, 1948. https://history.aip.org/history/exhibits/einstein /voice1.htm.

Campbell, Joseph. *The Hero's Journey: The World of Joseph Campbell: Joseph Campbell on His Life and Work*. United Kingdom: HarperSanFrancisco, 1991.

Campbell, Joseph. *The Hero with a Thousand Faces*. New York City, NY: Pantheon Books, 1949.

Chevalier, Barbara. *Keep Searching for Blue Jays: A Miraculous Account of Life beyond Our World: A True Story*. North Charleston, SC: CreateSpace, 2015.

Ekman, Paul. "An Argument for Basic Emotions." *Cognition and Emotion* 6, no. ¾ (1992), 169-200. http://www.paulekman.com/wp-content /uploads/2013/07/An-Argument-For-Basic-Emotions.pdf.

Featherman, Hannah. "Tree Profile: Aspen—So Much More Than a Tree." National Forest Foundation. March 21, 2014. https://www.national forests.org/blog/tree-profile-aspen-so-much-more-than-a-tree.

Hill, David. "Spiritual Alchemy for Beginners." Esoteric Meanings. October 21, 2016. http://www.esotericmeanings.com/spiritual-alchemy/.

King, Godfre' Ray. *Unveiled Mysteries.* Chicago, IL: Saint Germain Press, 1934.

King, Hobart M. "Goldstone." Geology. Accessed May 17, 2020. https:// geology.com/gemstones/goldstone/.

Knight, Stephen. *Merlin: Knowledge and Power through the Ages.* Ithaca; London: Cornell University Press, 2009. Accessed May 17, 2020. www .jstor.org/stable/10.7591/j.ctv75d4tw.

"Komodo Dragon." National Geographic. March 20, 2020. https://www .nationalgeographic.com/animals/reptiles/k/komodo-dragon/.

Montana, Cate. *The E-Word Ego, Enlightenment and Other Essentials.* New York City, NY: Atria Books, 2017.

"Phoenix: Mythological Bird." Encyclopaedia Britannica. Accessed May 17, 2020. https://www.britannica.com/topic/phoenix-mythological-bird.

Preston, Elizabeth. "It Only Takes Six Generations to Turn a Brown Butterfly Purple." Discover, August 8, 2014. https://www.discovermagazine.com /planet-earth/it-only-takes-six-generations-to-turn-a-brown-butterfly -purple.

Reeve, Christopher. *Still Me.* United States: Ballantine Books, 1999.

"Scorpions." National Geographic. September 24, 2018. https://www .nationalgeographic.com/animals/invertebrates/group/scorpions/.

Tigg, F. N. R. "Amber Guyger Sentenced to 10 Years in Prison." Complex. Complex Networks. October 3, 2019. https://www.complex.com /life/2019/10/amber-guyger-sentenced-to-10-years-in-prison.

# Acknowledgments

I wish to express gratitude to so many people that inevitably someone will be left out. Leaving people out is something this empath loses sleep over. For that reason, I have chosen to keep my acknowledgments broad. Thank you to:

∞ My family for loving me through hard times. Many of those difficult times shaped the course of my life and need for this book.

∞ Llewellyn Worldwide for believing in the message and for all of your hard work.

∞ The SoulTopians from staff to customers that encouraged and supported me through the fire of transmutation.

∞ My many friends and mentors in the tarot, divination, and wellness community for providing support and insight.

∞ Most of all, the people who choose not to support me. Thank you! You have helped me learn to transmute energy. I'm still working on it. But I know we are one, and I wish you love.

# Index